AURA GARDEN GUIDES

David Holloway

Decking

Practical advice on creating decking features in the garden

AURA BOOKS

Aura Garden Guides

Decking
David Holloway

© 2002 Advanced Marketing (UK) Ltd.,
Bicester, England

Produced by:
Transedition Limited for
Aura Books, Bicester
and first published in 2002

Editing by:
Asgard Publishing Services, Leeds

Typesetting:
Organ Graphic, Abingdon

Picture credits
Board Walk 11t, 11bl, 36, 38–9, 52, 54, 72b;
Richard Burbidge 58t; Cuprinol 2–3, 68–9, 70t,
71t, 75t; Forest Garden 4–5, 11br, 16, 30, 35, 37,
49, 58b, 60, 67, 74, 78–9; Liberon 75b; Ronseal
69br, 70–71; Timber Decking Association 50,
72–3, 73t, 76–7; John Trowell 8–9; Wickes
Home Improvement Centres 6–7, 47, 53, 61,
62–3, 64–5, 66, 73b

All drawings by Colin Fargher,
Fargher Design, Douglas, Isle of Man.

10 9 8 7 6 5 4 3 2
Printed in Dubai

ISBN 1 901683 98 2

David Holloway is one of the country's leading DIY writers. A qualified engineer, he devised, set up and edited *Handyman Which?*, the DIY and gardening magazine published by the Consumers' Association, and has contributed to nearly all the major home improvement magazines. He has written several books and, in recent years, has increasing turned his attention to the constructional side of gardening.

David enjoys the challenge of working with both natural and man-made materials, and relishes the opportunity of writing about technical and practical matters in down-to-earth, but not necessarily simplistic terms.

The two-level deck and balustrade, both stained with golden maple, make the ideal setting for a variety of pot and tub plants.

CONTENTS

All decked out

A timber deck performs exactly the same function as a paved patio area — a 'bridge' between house and garden and somewhere you can sit in comfort to enjoy the sun, enjoy the view of the garden, eat, read or just relax.

Timber decking is commonplace in North America — not surprising, since timber is widely available there. But there is one significant reason for the use of decking in North American houses that sadly doesn't apply in the UK — namely the widespread use of basements. A typical North American house will be built on top of a huge basement that may incorporate a garage, a workshop, an office and a playroom for the children, as well as a utility room and storage areas. So the living space is normally on the first floor, and to extend this out into the garden requires a high-level platform for which decking is ideal.

But timber decking is becoming more and more popular in this country as an alternative to hard paving. It has four big advantages:

• It can be used on sloping sites without the need to level the ground.

• It doesn't need major foundations (though posts need to be properly anchored).

• Wood is quieter, more attractive, more natural and easier to keep clean than paving.

• Decking is much more flexible than paving, allowing shapes to be made more easily and the surface to be on more than one level.

In this book, we look at the different ways to use decking in the home garden, describe the various components needed to build your own decking, and show you how they are put together.

The first part of the book looks at decking basics — including the tools, materials and equipment you need, planning and

preparation (including clearing the ground), providing supports, and cutting and fixing timber.

The second part (starting on page 30) gives step-by-step instructions for specific decking projects.

Using the book
To get an idea of the type of decking you might want, have a look at the contents list for the projects covered, glance at the various photo-

This deck has several interesting features — such as a fine balustrade and wide steps leading to the garden — but note the interest created by varying the pattern of the decking boards.

(and to avoid repetition) we have used cross-references to take you to the part of the book where the technique is covered in detail.

We have tried to keep jargon to a minimum, but if there is a word that you don't know, you will find the glossary on page 76 useful.

Timber in the UK is now universally sold in metric quantities and we have used these throughout — though it has to be said that many carpenters and timber suppliers still think in imperial (inch) sizes, so that if you ask for some 'four by two' you will get timber that is roughly 4×2 in — in fact 100×50 mm. Elsewhere, we have used metric quantities first, giving the imperial equivalent second. If you are not familiar with metres, centimetres and milli-metres, the best idea is to have a tape measure marked with both, and then you have your own ready-made converter.

Picking a project

If you are new to this kind of work, it would probably be best to go for a simple deck laid directly on the ground, levelling the ground beforehand if necessary. Elevated decks are much more complicated and require more skill to build safely and correctly.

Buying materials

You can buy decking from a DIY store or from timber merchants, but in either case you should have it delivered (the same applies to materials for making concrete).

Timber merchants may seem a bit intimidating at first, so it is best to go armed with the details of exactly what you want. You will find it best to get hold of a copy of the supplier's catalogue, so you can plan your decking in detail before going shopping. Most decking suppliers also have their own website where you can check out the materials available.

graphs throughout the book or look at the 'gallery' of decking ideas on pages 72–5. You don't have to construct a deck exactly like one of ours — you may perhaps be sufficiently inspired to design your own, using elements from different designs.

Although each of our projects is different, many of the same basic principles and tech-niques apply. For example, cutting and fixing decking boards is the same, however grand or modest your design might be. For this reason

What is decking?

At its simplest, timber decking is outdoor floor-ing — parallel timber boards running one way supported on joists running the other. But there are several important differences:

- The boards used in decking are narrower and thicker than normal floorboards and need to be specially shaped (rounded) at the corners to allow rainwater to run off more easily.

- The boards may be ribbed or grooved along the top to provide grip for walking on — particularly important when they are wet — and may be reeded on the bottom to improve both ventilation and drainage.

- The boards are laid with small gaps (typically 6 mm or $^1/_4$ in) between them
    - to allow for expansion and contraction
    - to provide ventilation
    - to improve drainage
    - to enable the decking to be swept clean more easily.

- The joists (or joist framework) are supported in some way by the ground rather than the walls of the house — though one side of decking next to the house may be attached to a timber beam on the house wall.

- All the timber used in decking must have been pressure-treated with preservative so as to prevent decay.

The decking can have steps leading up to it, or steps leading from one section to another. It can also be fitted with balustrading for both looks and safety (balustrading is essential on elevated decks). Decking need not be plain wooden boarding — you can add planters, water features, seating, pergolas, trellises, sand pits, spa baths and many other features.

There are several different decking patterns you can use, by arranging the boards in various different ways. Moreover, the decking itself can consist of squares, rectangles, triangles or even curved shapes.

Where to put decking

Normally, decking will be put in the same place as a patio — that is, on the sunny side of the house. To avoid having to seek planning per-mission, it should not be closer than 20 m (66 ft) to a main road or more than 3 m (9 ft 10 in) in height. But a deck does not have to be next to the house, and there are several points to bear in mind when considering where to place your deck for best effect:

Having several decks at different levels provides all sorts of possibilities — from excitement for children to stunning flower and plant displays. Each deck uses the one below it for part of its support.

this height (plus any balustrading) spoil the view from inside the house?

• Will the decking be safe for unsupervised children to play there? In particular, will you be able to see them?

• Will the decking be overlooked by neighbours or from the road? Bear in mind that neighbours may object if raised decking overlooks their garden.

• Will the decking interfere with any of the household services? In particular, will it make access to the drains more difficult?

DIY or professional installation?

This book shows you in detail how to construct your own low-level decking, using the DIY components widely available and based on the instructions from those component suppliers, most of whom can provide additional advice and technical back-up. But there are many suppliers of decking who offer an installation service in addition to supplying the decking — and you may decide, after seeing what is involved, that you would prefer not to do the actual work yourself.

You should certainly not attempt your own decking installation if your DIY skills do not already run to jobs like putting up shelving or erecting fencing, and you should always seek professional help if you want decking more than 60 cm (2 ft) off the ground, where structural considerations start to play a much greater role, and you will need to have an understanding of the Building Regulations.

But even if you decide that DIY is not for you, this book should give you some ideas of how you could use decking in your home — and arm you more effectively to deal with any professionals you may employ.

• Will it receive the sun at the times when you want it? Remember that south-facing walls will reflect heat.

• Will there be some areas of shade when the sun is at its highest? Will some areas be in shade all day?

• Will the decking be protected from prevailing winds, whether by fences, walls or buildings? If necessary, screening can be erected to provide a windbreak.

• What height does the decking need to be to provide the best view of the garden? And will

Tools and equipment

There are very few specialist tools you need to buy for installing decking, and you may already have at least some of the tools and equipment necessary. Even if you don't, it will normally be worth buying the tools listed here, as many will be useful for other DIY jobs around the home. Some things, like a builder's square, can be made up from spare pieces of timber; one tool that might be worth hiring is a cement mixer if you are setting a lot of posts in the ground.

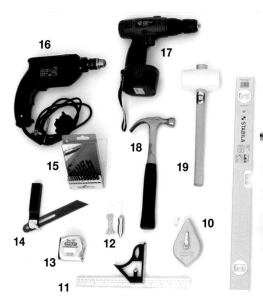

Tools to buy

As with anything else, you get what you pay for, and it is probably worth paying that little bit extra for good-quality tools if you want your decking to be level, your cuts to be square and your decking to look good.

First you will need some garden tools for preparing the ground — typically a pickaxe, a spade and a rake; the spade will also be needed for digging holes to take concrete for posts if that is how you are supporting your decking.

Some kind of saw is needed for cutting up timber. A powered circular saw will be quicker than a handsaw (panel saw) for making long, straight cuts, but if you want to make curved cuts, you will probably need a powered jigsaw. A plane (perhaps an electric planer) will be useful for trimming or levelling timber, and woodworking chisels for cleaning up joints.

One tool that is absolutely essential is a spirit level to get decking horizontal or just off the horizontal (a very slight slope is needed to allow rainwater to drain). Basically, the bigger the spirit level the better, but a sensible size is around 60 cm (2 ft) because it can be used for lots of other jobs as well. For setting out levels at more than this distance, the spirit level can be rested on a straight and true length of timber.

Other measuring and marking tools that you need include a retractable steel tape measure (a good length is 5 m or 16 ft), a chalk line, a com-

bination square and a sliding bevel (for marking saw cuts on wood). A plumb bob — a brass bob on a string — is essential if you want to erect elevated decking or decking on a sloping site, where it is used to mark the position of the supporting posts for the joist framework.

You will need an electric drill and normal twist drill bits for drilling clearance holes to take screws and nails and (with masonry drill bits) for making holes in the house wall to take a timber support. This drill could be cordless (battery-operated), but an extra cordless drill is useful as a powered screwdriver to speed up the tiresome process of putting in (and, sometimes, taking out) wood screws with a hand-operated screwdriver. Spanners are needed for nuts and bolts — a metric socket set is ideal. Having one or more quick-release clamps allows you to secure timbers temporarily — for example, whilst you drill them.

A hammer is needed for driving nails home, and a rubber mallet will be useful if you are laying paving slabs to support the decking or using decking clips to secure decking boards.

You will also need a timber straight-edge for levelling (with a spirit level), though the chances are that you will be able to use a length of decking board, which can be guaranteed to be straight and true. Wooden pegs will be needed for levelling ground and can be made from pieces of scrap timber (buy a length of 38-mm square timber and cut it up if necessary); you may need to make up some batter boards for setting out decking on a slope.

Tools to hire
The only things you really might need to hire are a cement mixer for mixing up concrete and a (hand-operated) post-hole digger.

Below *Tools that you can make up for yourself.*

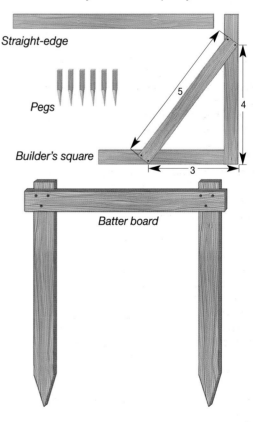

Above *Tools to buy:* **1** *panel saw;* **2** *circular saw;* **3** *jigsaw;* **4** *planer;* **5** *quick-release clamp;* **6** *chisels;* **7** *screwdriver;* **8** *spanner;* **9** *spirit level;* **10** *chalk line;* **11** *combination square;* **12** *plumb bob;* **13** *steel tape measure;* **14** *sliding bevel;* **15** *twist drill bits;* **16** *electric drill;* **17** *cordless drill;* **18** *hammer;* **19** *rubber mallet*

Tools to make
One tool you will probably have to make for yourself is a builder's square to provide a means for setting out the corners of your decking to exact right angles. You can make use of the mathematical fact that a triangle with sides in the ratio 3:4:5 will always have a right angle in it. So you simply join three pieces of straight wood with these ratios together, and you have a ready-made way of setting out 90° corners. A good size would be around 60, 80 and 100 cm — or, if you prefer working in inches, 24, 32 and 40 in. You could also make up other builder's squares: a triangle with a 30°, a 60° and a 90° angle has sides in the ratio 1:2:1·732, while a 45°/45°/90° triangle has sides in the ratios 1:1:1·414.

9

Decking materials

The most important thing about any of the wood that it used for outside decking is that it should be resistant to rot and woodworm infestation. A few woods (mainly the more expensive hardwoods) are naturally durable and resistant to such attack, but all other wood must be pressure-treated with preservative in order to protect it.

All reputable decking suppliers will provide timber that has been so treated, and they will also be able to provide decking preservative that you can apply to any cut ends as you install the decking.

Joists
The main framework to support the decking will normally be made from 50 × 150-mm preservative-treated sawn softwood. Where decking suppliers make other garden

structures, such as pergolas or arbours (not uncommon), they may also make use of existing components to provide support for decking.

The same size of timber is generally used for bearers, where these are used to fit under the joists, for noggings that can be fitted between the joists, and for ledgers (bearers or joists attached to the house wall).

Posts
The normal size of post used for supporting decking joists is 100 mm (4 in) square, which is also the standard size used for fencing. This, too, will be preservative-treated sawn softwood.

The basic decking structure made up of joists, posts and decking boards

Decking boards
As you might expect, it is with the decking boards themselves that you find differences between one supplier and another, since the material chosen (and its size) will affect the strength and appearance of the deck.

The most common finished sizes of decking board are:
- 140 × 38 mm ($5^1/_2$ × $1^1/_2$ in)
- 140 × 28 mm ($5^1/_2$ × $1^1/_8$ in)
- 112 × 38 mm ($4^3/_8$ × $1^1/_2$ in).

However, you may find other sizes available.

Note that these are the *actual* dimensions, which is the size after the sawn timber has been planed. You may find sizes quoted as the *nominal* dimensions — e.g. 150 × 50 mm — which are the rough-sawn sizes.

Western red cedar is a good choice for decking boards. It is a naturally durable softwood, has a nice straight grain and has little moisture movement. Its tannin content may tend to discolour ferrous (iron and steel) components, but it otherwise looks really good.

You may also find yellow cedar plus a selection of other softwoods, including redwood, Douglas fir and southern pine, all of which, however, need to be pressure-treated with preservative.

Hardwoods — such as oak and teak (a traditional timber for decking) — are naturally very durable and provide considerable strength when used for decking. Their main draw-

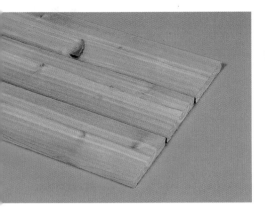

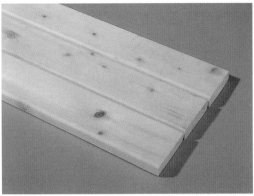

back is their price, but they are unequalled for attractiveness. On the down side, oak can split on the surface and may also be badly affected by ferrous components.

Preservative treatment

You will find the process called many things (suppliers all have have their own pet names), but the key letters to look for in preservative-treated timber are CCA — chromated copper arsenate. This is a water-borne preservative that is forced into the timber by an industrial pro-

cess involving combinations of vacuum and high-pressure cycles. It is vital for this to be carried out correctly — in particular for the wood to be properly dried both before and after treatment — so is not something you could dream of attempting yourself.

Surface treatment with preservative (by brushing or dipping) gives no more than short-term protection, but nevertheless is the only option you have at home for treating the cut ends of decking boards, joists and other timbers.

*Among the best softwoods for decking boards are Western red cedar (**left**) and Alaskan yellow cedar (**right**).*

There are various decorative treatments you can use for decking, some with anti-fungal and water-repellent properties, to make it look more attractive and stay looking more attractive (see page 68).

*Other refinements include decking squares (**left**), again in Western red cedar, and specially profiled decking boards (**right**).*

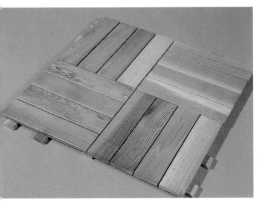

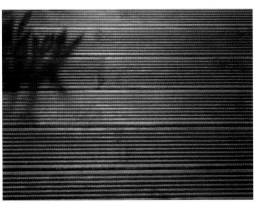

Supporting decking

There are six main ways in which you can support the framework that holds the decking boards:

1 Directly on the ground

2 On paving slabs

3 On concrete blocks

4 On posts secured into the ground

5 On posts secured to a hard surface

6 Attached to the house wall.

Methods **1** to **3** should be used when you're laying decking on a roughly flat surface, or one that will be flat after a small amount of excavation.

Methods **4** and **5** should be used when the decking is elevated, either to get it all off the ground, or because the ground is sloping so that one end of the decking is on the ground.

If the decking is to be next to the house, one end may also be supported directly on the house wall (**6**).

The decking itself needs only a very slight slope — say 1:150 — to allow for drainage, but the ground underneath should always slope away from the house, so that rainwater passing through the decking is carried away safely. A good slope for this is 1:40.

Directly on the ground

This is probably the least satisfactory option, though it is recommended by at least one decking supplier.

The ground clearly needs to be levelled first (see **Preparing the ground** on page 19) and you should put down a good layer of gravel (pea shingle), so that the joist framework has something to bed down on that is free-draining.

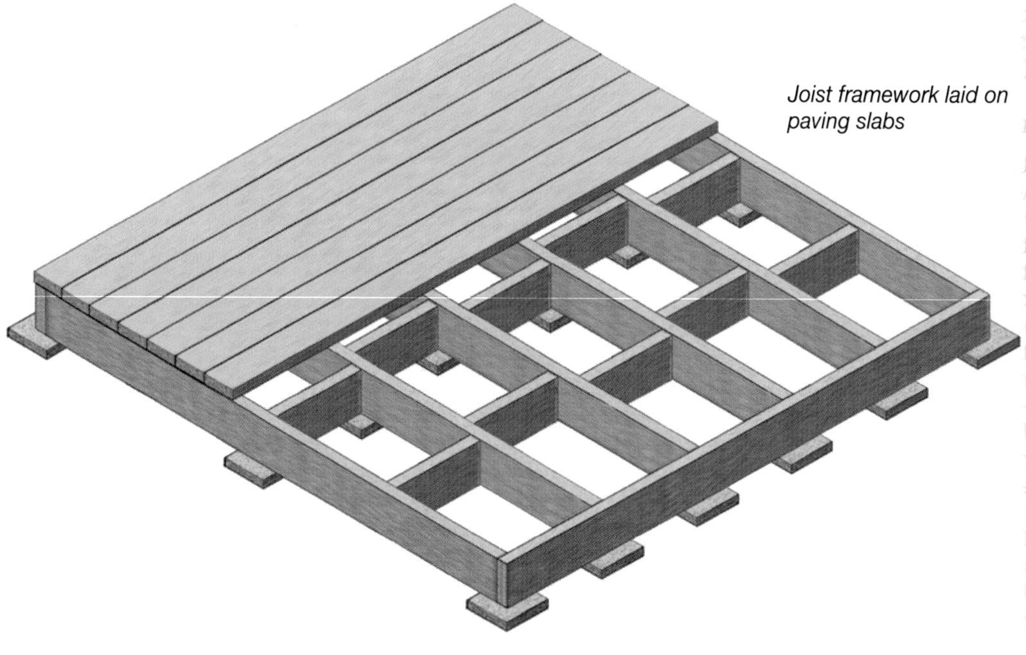

Joist framework laid on paving slabs

On paving slabs

This method is fairly common — the same method is used for supporting garden buildings, such as sheds. What matters is that the concrete paving slabs themselves should be level — or laid with a slight 'fall' from one to another to achieve drainage on the deck.

Once the ground has been cleared and black polythene sheeting has been laid over the surface, small amounts of sand — up to about 25 mm (1 inch) thick — are put down at each slab position. The slabs can then be lowered into place, and sand can be added or removed as necessary to get the correct height.

The illustration below left shows a joist framework laid on paving slabs.

On concrete blocks

There are two ways you can use concrete blocks to support your decking framework: one is by using concrete made *in situ*; the other is by using pre-cast concrete blocks (see overleaf).

On concrete blocks *in situ*

Using *in situ* concrete is hard work. You have to dig a hole, construct timber shuttering to support the concrete whilst it sets, level all the shuttering, mix the concrete — one part cement to four parts combined sand/aggregate by volume plus water — and tamp it into the hole. Then allow the concrete to set, remove the shuttering and finally backfill (with gravel or hardcore) in the gaps left by the shuttering. If the concrete is to have a slot that will support a decking joist, you will need to mount a removable timber block in the setting concrete to create this; alternatively, a steel mounting plate can be bolted down onto the concrete or set into the wet concrete. And you need to do all this at every support point!

On pre-cast concrete blocks

Using pre-cast concrete supports is much easier. These come with a slot already cut to take a joist and they simply sit on the ground. They are designed to be used on ground that has been levelled, though you can make slight adjustments by putting them on a sand bed (and adding or removing sand as necessary), or by putting slivers of timber (no more than 30 mm; $1^{1}/_{4}$ in) in the slot under the timber joists. Cleverly, some pre-cast concrete blocks also have a hole that can be used to mount a support post vertically for decking on uneven or sloping ground, or for elevated decking.

On posts secured into the ground

If you have ever erected a fence, you will probably already know about concreting timber posts into the ground. You use exactly the same procedure for the posts to support decking, although the posts are obviously a lot shorter. Once the concrete has been mixed (using dry pre-mixed concrete plus water is simpler than buying the separate ingredients), it is packed in around the post and sloped at the top to allow rain run-off. You will want to get the height of the top of the post correct before adding the concrete: there's not much you can do later if it is too low, but if it is too high, you can obviously trim the post with a saw.

On posts secured to a hard surface

you want to lay decking on an existing hard
urface — typically concrete — you can use
he type of fence post support that is
esigned to be bolted down. This has a flat
ange supporting a square socket, and the
ange has four holes to take bolts — so you
an attach wall anchors to the concrete after
ou have drilled suitably large holes with an
lectric drill fitted with a suitable large
nasonry drill bit.

Attached to the house wall

ecuring decking to the house wall is ideal if
he decking is slightly elevated. If the joists
un parallel to the house wall, the first one can
e secured to it using screws and wall plugs
r wall anchors. If the joists run at right angles,
 timber support beam can be secured to the
vall. This will either fit under the joists or it will
e fitted with galvanised joist hangers (like
nose used for ceilings in house con-
truction) to take the joists.

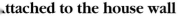

ven if the joist or wall support beam
edger) is preservative-treated (as it
hould be), it is still important to have
 gap behind it to allow for ventilation,
o that it can dry out if it gets wet. One
vay to do this is to fit washers to the screws
r bolts, so that the bearer is spaced around
0 mm ($^3/_8$ in) away from the wall.

he alternative — a more professional way of
olving the problem — is to insert some con-
nuous lead or zinc flashing into the mortar
oint on the wall above the timber ledger and
o fashion this over the top of the ledger to
eep rainwater off.

15

Planning and preparation

Once you have decided where your deck should be, what style you want and roughly what size it needs to be, you need to plan it in detail and prepare the ground.

What size deck?

You need to think of the size of the proposed deck in relation to the size of both the house and the garden. A large deck stuck on a small house and taking up a lot of garden will look totally out of place, whilst a tiny deck on a large house in a large garden may look like an obvious addition rather than something that blends in.

Decking is no different from any other home improvement: the aim should be to make an extension or conversion look as though it was actually part of the original house.

If you can, take a photograph of the proposed site and super-impose the decking on it. This way, you can see how it relates to existing garden features such as a pond or pool, trees and shrubs, or other timber garden structures such as sheds or pergolas. Remember that you may be able to 'soften' the effect of a large deck by having it on different levels, by

As part of the planning process, you could take a photo of where you intend to have the decking.

having a main deck linked to smaller sub-decks and so on.

If you plan to have a table and chairs for eating out on the deck, you will need a space of at least 2.5 m (8 ft 6 in) square, plus room to move around this. One answer could be to build a permanent bench seat into the edge of the deck-ing (perhaps incorporating it in a balustrade) so that the table can come right up to it; the table could be a permanent feature, too — especially if you fit permanent seating round three sides of it.

Deck height

You should already have con-sidered how the height of the decking is affected by the view you will get from it and the view that your neighbours may

have of it, but there are some more practical considerations.

First, is the garden lower than the main living room from which you will want to approach the decking? The decking will certainly feel more like part of the house if it is at the same level as the main living room, and perhaps may be approached via French windows or a patio door.

Second, does the garden slope away from the house? — and if so, what will the height of the decking be at its furthest point? (Remember that you will need professional help if the decking is more than 60 cm or 2 ft above the ground.)

An additional consideration is what will happen in the space under the decking. Potentially, this is useful storage space, provided it is accessible and well waterproofed — and you may well want to raise the deck slightly to make the best use of this space.

Decking patterns

Because of the necessary gaps between adjacent decking boards, the direction in which the boards are laid will have a significant effect on its appearance. There are six methods of laying decking, though you can combine one or more of these in a single deck.

Different patterns entail different amounts of cutting of boards and an essential tool for some patterns will be a combination square for marking and cutting at either 45° or 90°.

Chevron

Essentially a combination of diagonal layouts, dividing the deck into strips and laying alternate strips at 90°. Double-thickness joists are needed where board ends meet.

Herringbone

A bit like chevron in that the deck is divided up into strips, but the joints are square rather than angled and the pattern may be laid on diagonal joists. Again, double-thickness joists are required where the board ends meet.

Straight

With all the boards laid parallel to one of the main edges and at right angles to the supporting joists. This gives you two options: with the boards running either parallel to the house or at right angles to it.

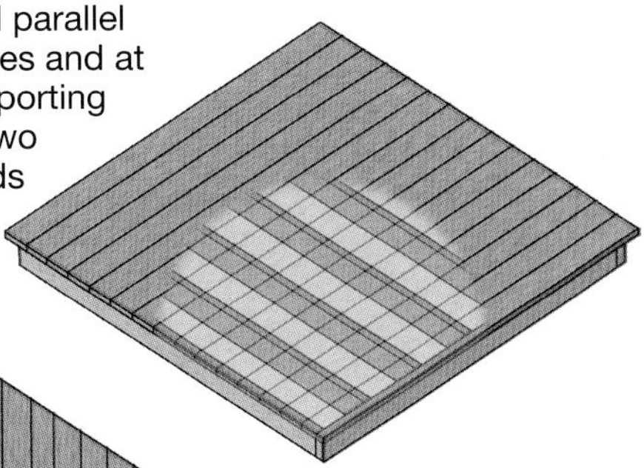

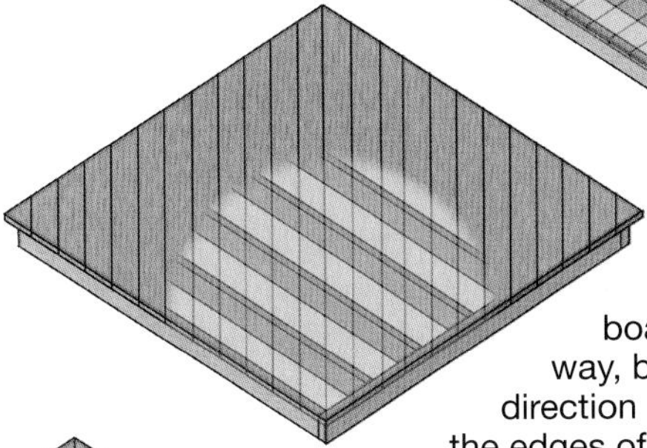

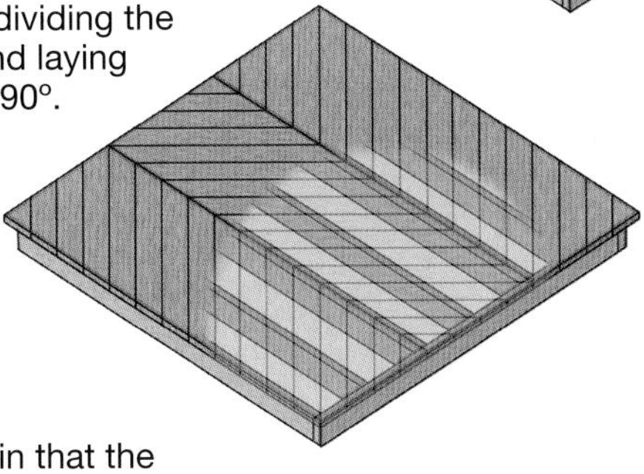

Diagonal

Again, all the boards run the same way, but at 45° to the direction of the joists and to the edges of a rectangular deck.

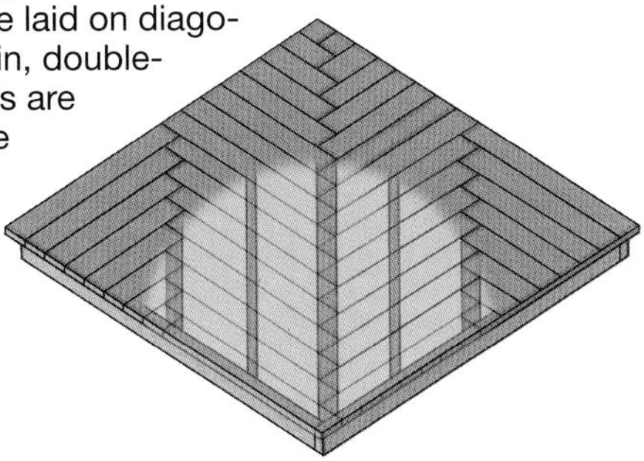

Other decking patterns

There are two other patterns that require a more complex structure and are less desirable for the beginner:

Basketweave. Here, the deck is divided up into squares, with alternate squares laid at right angles to one another. Half of the squares will need additional noggings (cross pieces) nailed between the joists to support the boards. If you want this pattern, consider buying pre-cut decking panels which will make the task easier.

Diamond Similar to basketweave in that the decking is divided up into squares, but two different diagonal patterns are used; no additional noggings are required.

Making a plan

It's best to draw a scale plan of your decking. A good scale to use for this is 1:20, where 1 metre on the ground is represented by 5 centimetres on paper. You can make life easier for yourself by using prepared graph paper.

As well as making the decking look the way you want it to, you will need to think about the number of boards, joists and supports you will need. This will mean thinking about:

- the spacing of the joists
- the spacing of the joist supports (slabs, posts, bearers or concrete blocks)
- the spacing of the boards themselves.

All of these depend on the sizes of the decking boards and support joists used, and on the type of timber they're made from.

Board spacing

Working this out is relatively easy (see panel below). You need a gap of at least 6 mm ($^1/_4$ in) between the boards. You can have gaps a little larger than this — perhaps up to 10 mm ($^3/_8$ in) — but you should bear in mind that small people's toes can get caught in larger gaps, and you are also more likely to lose small objects such as rings or coins down the gaps.

 Board spacing

For straight patterns you can work out the exact total width (across the boards), allowing 6 mm for each gap, using the following simple formula:

W = nw + g(n–1)

where
W = the overall width of the deck (in millimetres)
n = the number of boards
w = the width of each board
g = the gap width.

Now suppose you wanted a deck 3 m (3000 mm) wide made up of 141-mm boards with a spacing of 6 mm. Using the formula, you could have either 20 boards to give 2934 mm or 21 boards to give 3081 mm. If you wanted exactly 3 m, you could have 20 boards with the gap increased to 9.5 mm.

The calculation is more complicated for diagonal decks, but is less critical, since all the boards have to be cut at both long and short edges. If the decking is laid at 45° to the joists, the angled length of a 141-mm board exposed on each edge will be 199 (141 × 1.414) mm, whilst the angled gap will be 8.5 (6 × 1.414) mm. For boards laid at 30° to one edge (and therefore 60° to the other), the equivalent dimensions on the 30° edge will be 282 mm and 12 mm (exactly twice the normal board and gap widths), while on the 60° edge they will be 163 mm and 7 mm — these numbers are obtained by dividing 141 (and 6) by 2 and multiplying the answer by 1.732. Thank you Pythagoras!

Joist spacing

This depends on the size of decking boards you are using. The standard recommendation is 400 mm (16 in) spacing between joists, but you may be able to go up to 600 mm (24 in) if you use the thickest (38-mm) boards. Check the instructions from your supplier.

Joist supports

The spacing of supports will depend on the size of joists you are using and the way the decking is supported. The standard recommendation varies from 1.5 m (for a flat deck on paving slabs) up to 1.8 m (for decks supported on posts and trimmers), but again you should check with your supplier.

How many boards?

Your plan should tell you how many supports and joists you need, and the number of boards necessary to achieve the correct spacing with the boards correctly placed at the two opposite straight edges.

As a guide, the number of metres of board you need is equal to the area of the deck in square metres divided by 7 (for 141-mm board) or divided by 9 (for 112-mm board). But remember that decking boards can vary slightly in width. You should make a final check on the board spacing by holding all the lengths of board you need stacked closely together against one edge of the deck, so that you can measure the total gap left before dividing it by the number of boards less one to give you your actual spacing.

Levelling the ground

The best way to level a site is to use timber pegs, which you can level one by one starting at the house. Use string lines on 'batter boards' to mark out the deck area, using your builder's square to set the corners; a simple string line spirit level can be used to set the strings horizontal if required.

Hammer in the first peg, before using a spirit level (or a spirit level and a batten) to set the height of the next peg — perhaps 1.2 or 1.5 m (4 or 5 ft) away. Remember to use spacers under the spirit level or batten to get

Preparing the ground

The first thing you'll need to do will be to clear the proposed site completely of all vegetation, digging out any shrubs and small trees and applying a proprietary weed killer. Any existing paving may need to be broken up and removed. If you are laying a ground-level deck, the ground itself may need to be levelled, always remembering that it should have a slight slope away from the house.

the drainage slope (away from the house) correct; continue like this until you have the whole site marked out. For large sites, a water level (a long plastic tube filled with water) will enable you to check levels across a large distance.

Once you have the pegs in place, you can add or remove earth until the site is a continuous slope, after which it should all be covered with a large sheet of heavy-duty black plastic to prevent weed growth, with the plastic weighted down by a 50-mm (2-in) layer of gravel.

batter boards

string lines (to be kept level)

A sloping site

Use batter boards and a spirit level as for a level site. Position the boards roughly where the support posts will be, so you'll know how long these need to be to get the deck level. When laying the black plastic membrane, you'll need to cut it to fit round any posts if they are mounted in the ground.

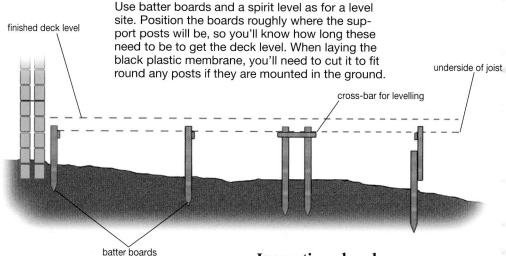

finished deck level

underside of joist

cross-bar for levelling

batter boards

Setting a fall

If you want to have a fall of, say, 1 in 40 on the site, to allow for drainage, you need to make up a spacer to fit under one end of your spirit level or batten. If the level is 60 cm long, this spacer needs to be 15 mm thick; if the batten is 1.2 m (4 ft) or 1.5 m (5 ft) long, the spacer needs to be 30 mm ($1^1/_4$ in) or 37.5 mm thick (the latter size is very close to 38 mm or $1^1/_2$ in — a standard sawn timber size).

The equivalent spacer sizes for a slope of 1:150 (for the decking) are 4 mm (for a 60-cm spirit level), 8 mm (for a 1.2-m batten) and 10mm (for a 1.5-m batten). You should be able to make suitable spacers up from strips of hardboard or thin plywood/MDF.

Most spirit levels should be accurate these days — but a professional will always 'end-to-end' each measurement, positioning the spirit level both ways round and, if necessary, taking the average of the two readings. If using a batten, you should double-check that it is true (by sighting along the bearing edge). Always use a batten with its longest dimension vertical — a good size is 150 × 50 mm (6 × 2 in).

Inspection chambers

If there is a drainage inspection chamber within the site of your proposed decking, you cannot simply cover it up — it must remain accessible so the drains can be cleared if they get blocked.

If the decking is elevated, there may be sufficient room to crawl underneath and still get to the inspection chamber, but ground-level decking will have to be built around it.

There are basically two ways round the problem. One option — much less attractive — is to raise the level of the inspection chamber cover with an additional frame, so that the cover is flush with the top of the decking and the decking boards are cut to fit around the inspection chamber cover. The other alternative is to fashion a removable (or hinged) hatch in the decking so that you can still get to the inspection chamber underneath. Either way, you will have to fashion the joist framework around the inspection hatch, using noggings spanning across two joists.

If you need to build over drains in this way, you should inform the Building Control Officer at your local council — he will want to be satisfied that your proposed solution meets the Building Regulations.

Cutting and fixing

When it comes to laying your decking, you will have to learn how to cut it accurately and then how to fix it.

Cutting decking

Decking is generally sold in 2.4-m (8-ft) or 3.6-m (12-ft) lengths, which may be either too long or too short for your deck. If it is too long, you will obviously have to cut it down to size; if it is too short, you may also have to cut it so that the cut ends meet over a supporting joist.

Some cuts in decking will need to be made with great precision — for example, the square ends necessary for a herringbone pattern, or where two lengths of decking meet over a joist, or the 45° cut necessary for diamond or chevron designs. Other cuts are less crucial before laying — especially the ends of a deck, where you might prefer to cut all the pieces slightly over length, trimming them to a perfectly straight line once all the decking is laid. You will almost certainly want to do this on a curved edge, or when laying one of the diagonal decking patterns.

The first golden rule with cutting timber is **measure twice and cut once**: you cannot put timber back once it has been removed!

There will be quite a lot of sawing to do, so it is worth setting yourself up with a proper saw horse, or a portable workbench, so that you can anchor the timber pieces properly and hold them firmly whilst you cut.

Combination square

A sliding bevel is a good tool for marking out angles on timber to be cut, but a more useful tool for decking is probably a combination square, which has both 45° and 90° settings (and usually a fine scriber point for marking), making it much more versatile than a carpenter's try square.

Panel saw

A good-quality panel saw can be used for cutting both decking and joists; once you have mastered the correct technique, you should be able to make good square cuts with little chipping.

Circular saw

A circular saw takes some of the hard work out of sawing, but is difficult to use accurately on small pieces of timber and is likely to chip the surface more.

Where it does come into its own, however, is for trimming the ends of laid decking boards in a straight line. If the edge lines up with the outer edge of a joist, the circular saw's rip guide can be set so that the saw cut is in the correct place and is kept there while you move along the joist; if the cut is beyond the joist, a straight timber batten can be used, clamped to the laid decking boards, to guide the sole plate of the saw.

Jigsaw

A jigsaw, like a circular saw, is very difficult to use on small pieces of timber, and is more difficult than a circular saw to keep on a straight line for trimming edges.

But a jigsaw comes into its own when you're trimming the ends of laid board in a curve. Take your time, because you are guiding the saw by eye (the second golden rule with sawing is **let the saw do the work**).

A random orbital sander can always be used for final finishing on gentle curves — the sanding plate is flexible enough to be adapted to a curve.

Preservative

After you've finished cutting, the timber, you should always remember to treat all the cut ends with additional preservative.

When you're cutting lengths before laying the decking, the simplest way to do this is to fill a bucket with preservative and stand the cut decking board in it, cut end down.

Fixing frames

The main supports for the decking boards are a series of joists, which for normal-size decking boards should be laid at aproximately 400-mm intervals. For some decks only joists need to be used, while for others you will want to fix noggings between the joists, and for elevated decks you will need to have supporting bearers below the joists.

As was explained on pages 12–13, the joist framework can be supported in a number of different ways: directly on the ground, on paving slabs, on concrete blocks, on posts secured into the ground, on posts secured to a hard surface, or attached to the house wall.

With some of these methods, you will need to secure parts of the framework together or secure the framework to posts.

Making a joist framework

When the joists are laid directly on the ground or on paving slabs, some suppliers recommend using a joist framework. This involves having timber members (trimmers) joining the ends of the joists, plus noggings fitted between the joists. Both measures will prevent the frame from twisting and thus give it more stability.

The most important thing — especially with noggings, which have to fit exactly between the joists — is that the ends should be cut exactly square. You can achieve this by marking all round the timber using a try square or combination square and then cutting carefully.

With noggings you also have to cut all the timber to the correct length: if you are using the first cut piece (which you are certain is right) to mark and cut the second piece, use this first piece to mark and cut all other pieces. If you use the second piece to mark and cut the third and so on, small errors could build up so that the tenth piece is much larger or smaller!

Once all the pieces have been cut to the correct length, all that remains is to screw or nail them together, using pilot holes for both nails and screws, and clearance holes with countersinks for screws.

Fixing to posts

Except with a very small deck, you won't want to fix joists to posts, as there would simply be too many posts. So, with an elevated deck or a deck on a slope, you use posts either to support a joist framework (see below) or to support bearers (see opposite) — normally of the same size timber as the joists, running under and at right angles to the joists.

The alternative for fitting joists or bearers to posts is to use one of the galvanised post caps available. These are screwed (or bolted) onto the top of the post, then screwed or bolted to the bearer or joist.

Fixing a joist framework

When joining a joist framework (joists, end timbers and noggings) to posts, the normal method is to make a lap joint at the top of the post, cutting away half of the timber to the depth of the joist, so that you can then bolt or screw through the post into the joist. At corner posts, you will have to cut the wood away from two sides to leave just a quarter of it showing.

Fixing bearers

Bearers for supporting joists can be joined in the same way, but a more secure fixing which does not involve cutting (and thereby weakening) the posts is to use a double bearer and fix bolts right through both beams, sandwiching the post in between. You will need a bolt at least 250 mm (10 in) long, plus washers to fit under both the bolt head and the nut; drill a hole of the correct size (typically 10 mm or $3/_8$ in) with all the timbers clamped together.

Fixing joists to bearers

You don't want the joists to be able to move sideways on the bearers. The normal recommended methods for securing them are joist hangers and joist connectors. Joist hangers are used where the top of the joist is flush with the top of the bearer, which is often the case when a bearer is fixed to the house wall. Joist connectors are used where the bearer is under the joist — a common situation with a deck on a sloping site, where just the far ends of the joists are supported by a bearer. The connectors, which are readily available in various shapes and sizes, are nailed to both the bearer and the joist.

Using a joist hanger

The galvanised joist hanger is nailed to the bearer and the end of the joist is simply dropped down into it before being nailed into place. Angled joist hangers are available for unusual deck layouts.

Fixing to the house wall

Where a ledger is fixed to the house wall, the best type of fixing to use is a wall anchor. This is a larger, more robust, version of a wall plug, and comes with its own bolt (fitted with a washer), for which you simply drill a hole in the joist or beam.

A larger hole will need to be made in the house wall, using an electric drill (mains or cordless) fitted with an appropriate size of masonry drill bit; hammer action on the drill will speed up the drilling process.

You should fit spacing washers on the bolt (to a thickness of around 10 mm) so that the beam or joist is set out from the wall to allow an air gap for drainage or ventilation. The alternative is to fit a flashing strip in the next mortar course up on the wall to keep the rain off, or to seal around the beam with silicone sealant.

The wall anchor bolts should be tightened but not over-tightened.

Fixing decking

There are three different ways of fixing decking boards to joists: nails, screws and ties. Every supplier has a favourite and some may suggest more than one method.

Nails are the easiest method, using two nails everywhere a decking board crosses a joist. But nails will be visible and you could damage the boards getting them in. To avoid splitting the wood, it is always best to pre-drill pilot holes for the nails. The nails themselves must be galvanised to prevent rust. 75-mm or 3-inch annular ring shank nails are usually recommended.

If you punch the nail heads below the surface, you could use a matching exterior wood filler to cover the heads, which could then be stained to match the remainder of the decking.

Screws require more work than nails, but they provide a neater finish, and are much easier to remove if a single

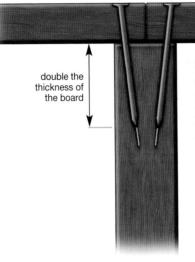

double the thickness of the board

Skew nailing

Where two decking boards meet over a joist, skew nailing is normally recommended — driving the nails in at an angle so that they can be set in from the ends of the boards to avoid any possible splitting.

decking board needs to be replaced. Pilot and clearance holes should be drilled (and countersunk) for the screws, which should be rustproof (stainless steel or zinc-plated).

The normal screw size recommended is the 75-mm (3-in) No 10, which needs a 5-mm

clearance hole in the deck sboard and a 2-mm pilot hole in the joist below. Some decking manufacturers can supply stainless steel screws with recessed square heads, which allow the twisting force to be applied more easily from the (special) screwdriver.

Fixing screws

Use two screws at each point where a joist supports a deck board.

Fixing screws

Where two boards meet over a joist, you can screw an additional timber member to the joist at that point so that the screws can be set in from the ends of the boards to avoid splitting.

Ties have the big advantage that the fixings are completely concealed — and there is no danger of damage to the decking surface, and no nails or screws protrude as a threat to bare feet.

The first row of decking boards is fixed using galvanised screws, but after that deck ties are used — are angled galvanised spikes, secured with a nail, with a second horizontal spike.

Using deck ties

The main spike is driven into the joist, with the deck tie up against the first length of deck board laid. The second length is then hammered into the horizontal spike (using a piece of scrap timber to protect the edge), with the deck tie maintaining the correct gap between the boards.

The recommended method is to have two people hammering at different parts of the board (using scrap timber to protect the board from damage), so that the board does not spring off one tie while being hammered onto another one. The last board is additionally screwed down.

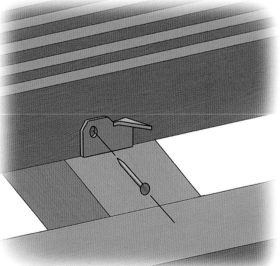

a deck tie

Getting the spacing right

You will want to have equal spacing between the boards for an attractive appearance, and the best way to achieve this is to use a physical spacer — either small strips of thin plywood for a 6-mm or 9-mm gap, or a home-made sliver for the gap of your choice (up to 10 mm).

Decking boards can vary slightly in size and it is possible that your calculations for board spacing might be slightly out. It is always best to lay the boards out tight together on the decking framework, with one edge lined up with the ends of the joists (or the outer edge of the trimmer), and measure the gap that remains. You then divide this by the number of boards less one to check on the actual gap you need between each board.

You certainly don't want to be in the business of having to plane boards down, though it might be possible at this preliminary stage to adjust the overall size of the frame. Double-check the gap size as you work (see illustration below).

Re-checking the gaps

After you've laid a few deck boards, measure the space left to fill and divide this by the number of boards left to lay. Subtract the board width to get the remaining gap width.

A ground-level deck

Over the next few pages, we tell you in detail how to plan and build a simple ground-level deck, using paving slabs to support the decking. You don't need to attach the decking to the house, though of course you may choose to.

How to do this, and how to build a similar deck if the ground is sloping, are both covered in the next project, starting on page 38.

Right *This is an ideal situation for a deck — south-facing, on flat ground, not overlooked and with good access from the house*

Below *The addition of a deck and balustrade panels, plus some furniture and accessories, completely transforms the area.*

Planning and preparation

This deck is straightforward as it runs virtually the full width of the house, minus around 400 mm (16 in) on either side. The decking boards are parallel to the house, so the main supporting joists are at right angles — and the deck can extend for as far as you want into the garden.

With a deck like this it's best to plan roughly where you are going to put the main furniture, and then experiment on the original ground to see how different sizes of deck feel,

efore deciding on your final
ze. Here we chose a deck that
as around 3.8 m (12 ft 6 in)
ide, using 26 decking board
idths. For details of how to fit
alustrades, see page 58.

If your ground is as level and
ouble-free as the one on the
ft, you are in for an easy ride,
nd all that will be necessary is
 remove the turf (perhaps
eeping it for use elsewhere in
he garden if it is good quality)
nd to dig out the soil to a
epth of around 100–150mm
4–6 in). You may well need to
attle with weeds, tree roots
nd the like in order to get
own to a proper surface.

Start by setting out the size
nd shape of the deck, using
atter boards and string (see
age 19). Remember that you
eed roughly half the width of
 paving slab extra on each
imension (the joists do not
ome right to the edge of the
utside slabs). The great thing
bout using a batter board is
hat it is easy to hammer into
he ground (outside the pro-
osed decking area), and then
ou can move the string lines

along it until you've achieved
the exact right angles you want
using your builder's square
(see page 9). Check that the
marked area is an exact rect-
angle (if that's what you want)
by measuring the two diago-
nals. They should be the same.

Now mark out the area to be
excavated, remove the turf and
dig out the topsoil. If while
you're doing this you find that
the string lines get in the way,
then mark the soil below them
with the tip of the spade blade
and remove them — but you
should if at all possible work
with them in place so that you
have a constant check on the
exact size.

Compact the soil surface at
the bottom of the rectangular
hole and ensure that it has a
slight slope away from the
house. You can do this by
using a spirit level and a long
batten (use one of the timbers
that will form the joist frame)
and positioning a spacer
underneath the far end
of the batten. Aim at
a slope of
around

1 in 40, and think about what
will happen to the water that
falls through the deck: ideally
you will be able to direct it into
a trench and lead it away to
one side of the finished deck.

Now lay a damp-proof mem-
brane (a sheet of thick black
polythene) and cover with
50 mm (2 in) of sand.

The paving slabs sit on the
sand with the joists on top of
them. The joists should be at
400-mm (16-in) or 600-mm
(2-ft) centres, depending on
the size of the decking boards
used, so it should be fairly
simple to work out how many
joists you need. With this type
of rigid frame you don't need
to support each joist. The slabs
can be placed around 1.8 m
(6 ft) apart in either direction,
always under a joist.

Lay the slabs as shown in the
illustration below. You won't
need any slope on the deck
itself, which means the slabs
furthest from the house will
need more sand beneath them.

aying the slabs

tart with the slabs
long the house wall
nd level these using
our long batten and
pirit level, adding or remov-
ng sand underneath them as
equired. Then you can use each of
hese to set out the remaining slabs, using
our spirit level and batten in more than one
irection to get all the slabs at the correct level.

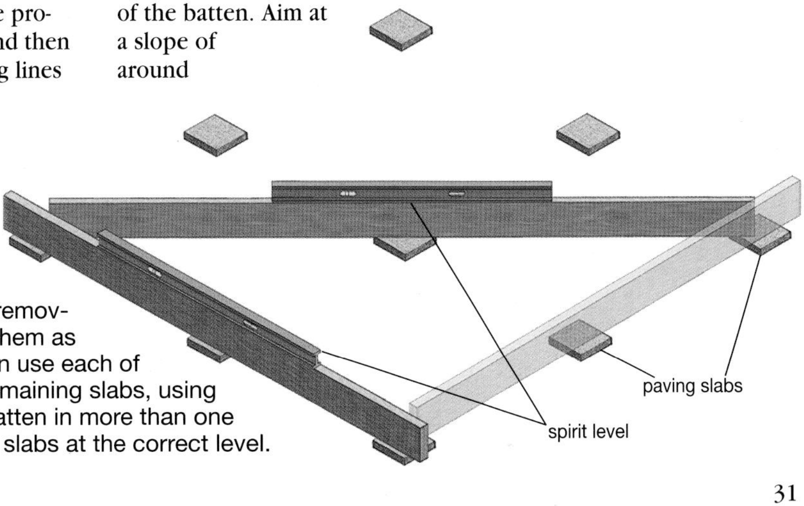

paving slabs

spirit level

Making up the frame

For this deck we have used a complete self-contained frame with a 'closing' end board (known as a trimmer) along the ends of the joists, all of which are equal in length.

If you do not want the cut ends of the trimmer to show, you could make the two outer joists longer — overall by twice the thickness of the trimmer. It all depends which way you will be looking at the deck — cut ends will always be visible on at least one side!

Cut all the joists first, making sure that the ends of each are square and that they are all exactly the same length, and then cut the trimmers to the length required; remember that the decking boards can overlap the edge joists and that the deck will look better if they do. If you are not totally confident about your ability to cut square and to length, the trimmers can be cut slightly oversize and trimmed after the frame is constructed, but you can't make them longer again. Before going on to the next stage, treat all cut ends with preservative (see page 11).

Now you can make up the basic frame by nailing all the pieces together — unless of course you want to use joist hangers (see page 25). Work out the length of the noggings (the joist spacing less the thickness of one joist) and cut all these to this size — check that they are all identical.

Nail the components together as shown in the illustration below, using galvanised nails. It will make life much easier if you pre-drill all the nail holes first: a clearance hole in the piece of timber through which the nail passes, and a (smaller) pilot hole in the timber into which the nail is secured.

You will have to stagger the noggings as shown in the illustration in order to to be able to fit them so that you can get the nails in.

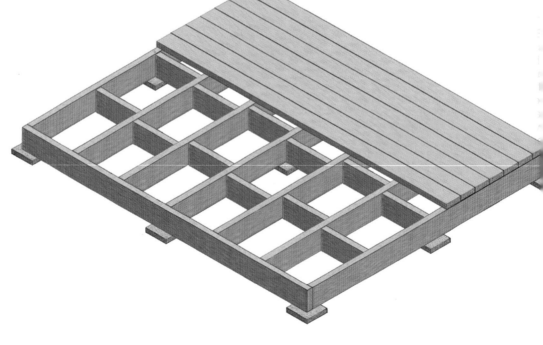

Fitting the decking

First of all lay down the number of boards you are using on the deck surface to check the spacing you will need. Measure the difference between the combined width of the boards and the overall width of the deck frame, and divide this by one less than the number of boards to get the exact spacing. With this design of frame (where there is a full-size end board) you can overlap the edge boards by up to 37 mm ($1^1/_2$ in) if this will help you to achieve a spacing of an exact number of millimetres — something between 5 mm and 10 mm. Make up one or more spacers for use when laying deck boards, using something like a large nail or a metric machine screw or bolt (conveniently labelled with their size) or an offcut of plywood or MDF, both of which come in suitable 6-mm sizes.

If the deck is longer than your lengths of decking board, work out where the joins in the decking board are going to be: the join must be over a joist, and it will look better if all the joins are not along the same joist. For our deck, we lined up the joins in every second strip, which gives a pleasing effect. But you may not be so lucky, so simply use the offcut from the end of one row to start the next row, finishing exactly in the centre of a joint. Don't worry about the exact overhang at the ends, since you are going to cut these boards down at the end anyway (though you obviously don't want to waste timber). Avoid very short lengths — the board should span at least three joists.

Before cutting boards, mark the cutting line all round the timber using a combination square (see page 21) and then ensure that you cut on the waste side of the line, keeping the saw cut as square as possible. Treat all cut ends with preservative.

Select the straightest decking board you can find to start with — the position of all the others will depend on this.

Levelling off

Before fitting the boards, check with a straight-edge that the tops of the joists are absolutely flat and level with one another — if necessary, use a plane to remove any high spots (an electric planer will make the task easier, but needs a lot of care in use).

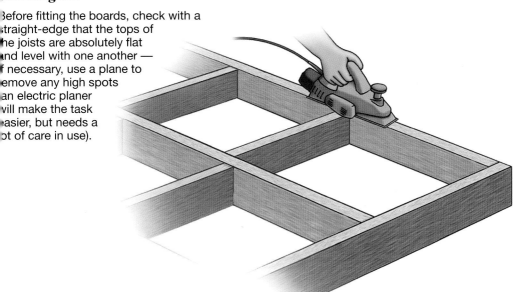

Fixing the decking boards

Drill clearance holes in the deck boards at each joist position and fix with two screws or two nails. Once the first row is fitted (allowing for a slight overhang if you want), make sure you use your spacers to position the next row exactly; you should be able to bend any out-of-true boards into line, provided you fit the nails/screws one joist at a time.

Do take time and trouble over this — the deck will look so much better if the boards are all exactly parallel and the fixing screws or nails are all exactly in line.

It will speed things up consider-ably if you drill pilot holes for the screws or nails in the joists and use a cordless drill/driver to put screws in. You can buy or hire an automatic nail gun, specially designed to take decking nails, but this is expensive and you may be happier sticking with a humble hammer.

It's worth looking at the way the end grain of each decking board runs. Assuming the board can be fitted either way round, fit it with the timber growth rings pointing down-wards (i.e. convex rather than concave). This will prevent 'cupping' of the boards (a curling at the edges).

Always use rustproof screws or nails — brass (screws only), galvanised (or zinc-plated) or stainless steel. At joins, angle the screws or nails towards the centre of the joist over which the boards meet.

When you get to around 1 m (3 ft) from the last edge, check the spacing again to see if you need to make any adjustment to the gaps between boards; you don't want to have to make it all up in the last gap.

Finishing off

Even if you have cut all the boards as carefully as you can, it is very unlikely that the ends will line up, so the final cutting task it to cut them all to a straight line. You can create a suitable line by 'snapping' a chalk line across the boards, allowing for an overhang beyond the last joist of up to 40 mm ($1^1/_2$ in) if required — no overhang if you are going to fit a decorative fascia board.

A circular saw is the best tool to use for finishing off boards in a straight line — and by far the easiest way of using it is to nail or clamp a straight timber batten down onto the decking boards, using this to guide the soleplate of the saw (see page 22). You can measure the amount this batten needs to be spaced away from your chalk line by measuring the distance from the soleplate edge to the saw teeth on the saw itself, but it's always best to have a trial run to get the exact spacing.

When using a circular saw for this purpose, it is very important to keep it pressed tightly against the batten all the way along the cutting line, which means you need a solid batten that is well anchored — and always take special care for the last few centimetres. Remove any rough edges from the cut ends and treat them with preservative.

Finally, the whole deck can be treated with stain, decking oil or water repellent (see page 68).

Easy-lay decking frame

To save you all the trouble of cutting up and making a joist framework, an easy-lay decking frame comes with the pressure-treated timbers already cut to size and pre-notched so that they fit together to create a solid foundation.

You are, of course, stuck with the sizes the manufacturer has decided on — the particular make shown here comes in just two lengths: 2.4 m and 3 m. On the other hand, the framework is incredibly easy to lay and ideal for use with deck tiles. The 3-m-square deck shown here takes exactly 36 50-cm-square deck tiles.

*Easy-lay decking frames are so simple to construct. Laying the deck base (**top**) simply involves slotting the components into place (**centre**) — and the final result (**bottom**) looks really professional.*

Using concrete block supports

An alternative way of laying ground-level decking is to use concrete block supports instead of paving slabs. The site needs to be cleared and levelled in much the same way, except that you don't need to excavate the ground: it should be sufficient just to rake the topsoil roughly level (or with a slight slope away from the house).

As with paving slabs, a ground-cover membrane should be used to discourage weed growth (applying a weed-killer first is often recommended), and the concrete blocks are simply laid on top of this at the recommended spacing. You can use a gentler drainage slope than with slabs — say, 1 in 100.

Concrete block supports can be used in two ways for ground level decks: either supporting the joists directly or supporting bearers which in turn support the joists.

If the blocks support the joists directly (as in the illustration below), you will need at least two blocks for every joist (at 400-mm or 600-mm centres depending on the size of decking

boards used). The maximum spacing between the blocks (for nominal 50 × 150-mm joists) is 2.9 m (for 400-m joist spacing) or 2.4 m (for 600-mm joist spacing).

If you use bearers, fewer concrete blocks will be needed, as the bearers can be 1.8 m apart (with blocks every 1.8 m along their length), but the decking will be 15 cm (6 in) higher off the ground.

The joist or bearer can extend beyond the support for a distance of up to a quarter of the spacing between supports: the load on this 'cantilever' section is balanced by the load between the supports.

Laying joists directly on concrete blocks

Skew nailing should be used where boards meet above a joist.

Minor differences of up to 30 mm ($1^1/_4$ in) in level between one block and the next can be made up with solid timber wedges inserted underneath the joists: the tops of the joists should be level as determined by means of a spirit level and a long straight wooden batten (see page 31). You should also plane down any high spots (see page 33) before fitting the decking boards.

The joists/bearers don't need to be secured to the concrete block supports, but if both bearers and joists are used, then you will need to secure the joists to the bearers using one of the methods described on page 25. Once the joists are in place, the decking is fixed in the same way as for the ground-level deck using paving slab supports (see page 34).

A ground-level deck can form the base for various add-ons such as a pergola (see page 62).

An elevated deck

Many decks in North America are built at what in the UK is called first-floor level. There is no reason why you shouldn't have a deck at this height if that's what you want, but don't try to build it yourself without considerable professional help! Not only will you need someone to design it for the correct strength, but the plans will also have to be passed by the local building control officer since Building Regulations will come into play.

Decks up to around 60 cm (2 ft) high should be OK, though even then you need to think about safety — especially with regard to elderly folk or small children, who could easily fall off the edge of the deck. Balustrades are covered on page 58, and handrails for stairs on page 56.

Building an elevated deck follows much the same procedure as building a ground-level deck, but you will need to know how to attach it to the house and how to mount the posts that support the joist frame. You may also need posts to support a staircase leading to the deck.

Planning and preparation

An elevated deck requires a little more imagination at the planning stage, since you cannot visualise it quite so easily as a ground-level deck. Read the section on page 16 to help you decide on the size and shape.

When planning the height, you need to be aware of the position of the damp-proof course of the house walls. This is an impervious barrier that is usually positioned two or three brick courses above ground level, and is there to prevent damp rising up the walls. Ground-level decks should ideally be at least 150 mm (6 in) below the DPC to prevent rain splashing up above it. Elevated decks with the house end on the ground should also be at this level, but elevated decks attached to the house wall should be above the DPC and *not* bridging it.

The ledger beam attached to the house wall can be used in one of three ways:

- as the first joist for deck boards running at right angles to the house wall
- as a support bearer under the joists for deck boards running parallel to the house wall
- as a support bearer, at the same level as the joists, for parallel decking, using joist hangers to connect the joists.

If it is the first joist, you will need posts and bearers to support all the other joists. If it supports the joists, you will need one or more support bearers to support the far end of the joists; the number depends on the size of the deck. If the ledger beam is used to support joists, you might want to fit a double thickness for extra strength, simply bolting two beams together and using longer bolts to secure them to the wall.

It is much easier to use bearers to support the joists. Using posts to support the joists directly means having at least one post per joist, whereas bearers need only one post for every 1.8 m or 2.1 m of bearer length (see table on page 42). Double bearers (fitted either side of the posts using galvanised bolts) are the best type to fit.

Clearing the site

It makes sense to start by marking out the site roughly and clearing the ground, removing all vegetation from under the deck position and creating a nice gentle slope away from the house. Apply a weedkiller to the ground to kill off all the weeds, and cut out the black plastic membrane that will be put in place under the deck.

The deck in this photo is attached to the house, with French windows leading out onto it. As the garden slopes away, the far end has been fitted with a balustrade and steps leading down to the garden.

Fitting the ledger beam

The starting point for setting out an elevated deck is the ledger beam attached to the house wall, so the first task (once you have decided on the overall deck size and drawn your plan) is to cut this to size and fix it to the house wall.

The vast majority of houses in the UK have masonry outer walls (even if the basic structure of the house is timber-framed); if your house has cladding of any kind (tiles, shingles or weatherboarding), it would be best to seek professional help as some of it will have to be removed so that the ledger can be fixed securely to the underlying framework. The alternative, of course, is to make the house end of the deck elevated as well, with posts spaced just away from the house.

For a masonry wall, the ledger is fitted with wall anchors, which are like large metal heavy-duty wall plugs, but come with their own 10-mm ($^3/_8$-in) hexagonal-headed bolts. For normal-size ledger beams (50 × 150 mm), you will need a pair of these every 60 cm (2 ft) along the wall, and the wall anchor should

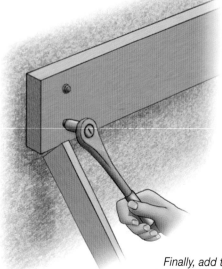

Finally, add the bolts and tighten them with a spanner.

go at least 100 mm (4 in) into the wall. Mark the holes and start by drilling 10-mm ($^3/_8$-in) holes for the bolts through the ledger beam.

Mark out the position of the ledger beam on the wall, using a spirit level on top of the proposed ledger to get it horizontal. This will be too heavy for you to manage on your own, so you will either need a helper or you will have to prop the ledger temporarily in place. A useful device (especially where you are running decking round a corner) is a water level. This is a long plastic tube containing water, which has a clear marked phial at either end. Because water always finds its own level, you can be sure that the two similar markings are exactly at the same height when the water is up to the two marks.

Once you have the position of the ledger marked out, use a pencil or a nail to mark through the bolt holes on to the wall behind. Remove the ledger and drill out the holes in the wall for the wall anchors, using the recommended size of masonry drill bit. Push or hammer the wall anchors home.

Before fitting the ledger to the wall, add some spacer washers to bring it about 10 mm ($^3/_8$ in) out from the wall. This will allow rainwater to pass down behind the beam. The alternative is to seal around the beam with silicone sealant and then mortar a lead or zinc flashing strip into the mortar course immediately above the ledger, dressing it down over the ledger.

Setting out the post positions

Once the ledger is in place, you can use it to set out the shape of the deck, and in particular, where the supporting posts will go.

Just as for a ground-level deck, you will need to use batter boards, a builder's square and string lines, perhaps with a line level (a small spirit level with hooks) on the strings to keep them horizontal. The string lines should be tied to nails put into the top of the ledger board if it is to be used as a support under the joists; to the bottom if it is to be a joist or a bearer to support the joist with joist hangers.

*Setting out the post positions is
the trickiest part of the job.*

You should always take time and trouble over this part of the process. You should already have worked out where the posts need to go — with a joist spacing of 400 mm (16 in), the joists need supporting only every 3 m along their length (see table overleaf), which gives you the number of bearers you will need. The joists can overlap the furthest bearer by 0.75 m (a quarter of the permissible span), so if your deck extends more than 3.75 m from the house wall, you will need two additional bearers; if it is more than 6.75 m from the wall, you will need three bearers, and so on. The bearers need supporting posts at no more than 1.8-m intervals along their length, with the posts equally spaced — but again, each bearer can project up to a quarter of the maximum span (i.e. 45 cm), so decks up to 2.7 m wide can be supported by two rows of posts.

Use additional strings tied to the batter boards to mark the post positions, measuring in from the corners so that two strings cross at each post. Make sure these strings are really tight. Intermediate posts positions can be marked by measuring along the string and applying a piece of adhesive tape to the string.

Now comes the tricky bit (see illustration), for which two people are best. Suspend a plumb bob (a pointed brass weight on a length of string) from the string junctions or marks corresponding to the post positions, so that you can locate the post position on the ground. Drive a small wooden peg into the ground at each post position. You might like to have the membrane in position whilst you do this, so that you can cut small holes in it and drive the pegs through these. Remove the membrane and enlarge the holes so that they will be big enough to take the posts later. Make a few drainage holes in the membrane at the same time.

Take the opportunity when marking the post position to measure the above-ground height of the post (from the ground to the string).

Mounting the posts

Digging holes for posts is hard work, not least to keep the sides of the hole straight — it's very easy to end up with a tapering hole. Unless you have served an apprenticeship in grave-digging, some mechanical help is a good idea. You can hire one of three types of post-hole borer: a large hand-operated auger type, a petrol-driven version of the same, or a clam-shell digger that is in effect two opposing spades and uses a scissor-like operation to make the hole; it also allows you to 'flare' the bottom of the hole, which will help to anchor the concrete.

Elevated deck design

using 50 × 150-mm joists on double 50 × 150-mm bearers supported on 100-mm-square posts

Deckboard thickness	Joist spacing	Bearer spacing	Post spacing
26–28 mm	400 mm	3 m	1.8 m
38–42 mm	600 mm	2.4 m	2.1 m*

*1.8 m preferred

Professional decking installers will normally use a concrete footing to mount a large screwed J-bolt, onto which they will later fit a galvanised stirrup that in turn supports the post. You will probably find it easier to mount the post directly in the ground, surrounding it with concrete. To do this with a 100-mm (4-in) square post, you will need a hole roughly 225 mm (9 in) square or round and 450–600 mm (18–24 in) deep — aim to have at least half the overall length of the post in the hole.

Once the hole has been dug, cut each post roughly to length (plus 200 mm for trimming) and place a large stone (or piece of concrete or 75 mm of gravel) in the bottom of the hole to help drainage. Put the post in place on top of this, supporting it with timber struts, using a spirit level to make sure it is perfectly vertical before packing mixed concrete in around it.

You will find it easier to buy bags of pre-mixed concrete (containing cement, sand and aggregate in the correct proportions); all you need to do is to add water, but don't make the concrete too wet. If you have a lot of posts, hire a cement mixer for the day;

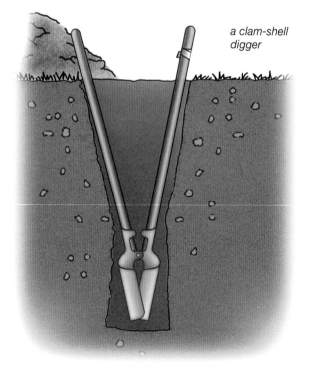

a clam-shell digger

llow one 25-kg bag of mixed
oncrete for each post.
  Repeat the process for all the
other posts and leave the
concrete to set. It would not be
a bad idea to nail some lengths
of timber between the posts to
keep them vertical whilst the
concrete sets. When it has
dried (leave at least 24 hours),
remove the struts and the
timber lengths. Replace the
black membrane, fitting it over
the posts, and cover it with a
50-mm (2-in) layer of gravel to
anchor it and aid drainage.

Completing the framework

You can now use a batten plus
a spirit level to mark lines on
each post. Rest the batten on
top of the wall ledger, set it
horizontal and mark each
post. Allow a slight
slope away from the
house (say, 1 in 150)
and measure down the
post by this amount
from the horizontal
line. If, for example,
your first posts are 3 m
(10 ft) from the ledger,
allow 20 mm (0.8 in).
  Continue the line all
around the posts. Then, if
the joists are to be supported
on top of the wall ledger, mark
a second line further down by
the width of the bearers you
will be using. If the joists are to
be supported by joist hangers
on the wall ledger (or if the
wall ledger is the first joist),
mark a third line a further
joist/bearer width down the

Nail some timber struts to each post while the concrete sets, having first ensured that the post is vertical

43

post. Using an offcut of the same size timber will save time.

Now you can fit the double bearers that will support the joists. Cut these to length, remembering that they can extend beyond the posts by up to 45 cm (18 in), and then mark the position of the posts on them, making sure you have an equal length of bearer going beyond each outer post. Mark two holes on the bearer at each post position for the bolts, one above the other, and place the bearers in position on the posts, aligning them with the lines you drew earlier. Secure temporarily with clamps (or some decking screws).

Now drill holes right though the first bearer, through the post and out through the other bearer, using a drill bit the same size as the bolt — use 10-mm ($^3/_8$-in) bolts, 250 mm (10 in) long. Take great care to keep the drill bit horizontal and square to the bearer.

Fix the bolts and nuts using a galvanised washer under the head of both the nut and the bolt. If you use coach bolts, you will not need the second washer.

Finally, use a panel saw (see page 22) to cut off the tops of the posts flush with the tops of the double bearers. To keep water out, gun some silicone sealant around the bolt heads and nuts, and into any gaps between the posts and bearers.

Fixing the joists

Start by marking the position of each joist on the wall ledger and the support bearers, remembering that the joist spacing should not exceed 400 mm for 28-mm thick boards, or 600 mm for 38-mm thick boards. At each joist position, mark the outline of a joist hanger and then fit all the joist hangers to the ledger beam using galvanised nails. With some types of joist hanger, you will need a spacer of the joist material (a short offcut will do) to position the joist hanger correctly.

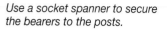

Use a socket spanner to secure the bearers to the posts.

Secure the joists in the joist hangers with galvanised nails.

Skew nailing (see page 27) is one way of fixing the joists to the bearers.

Cut all the joists to length and lay them in the joist hangers and across the support bearers. However, before nailing them in place at the joist hangers, line the joists up on the marks on the bearers to make a visual check that they are parallel and evenly spaced.

Where the joists cross the bearers you have two choices. One is simply to skew-nail down through each joist into the bearer below — something that will be a lot easier if you drill angled pilot holes in the joists first. The other is to use a galvanised bracket, secured with nails to the face of both the bearer and the joist.

Cutting timber

Whenever you cut timber, whether for posts, joists or deckboards, smooth off the rough edges with something like a rasp, and treat the cut end with preservative.

When cutting timber that has been CCA-preservative-treated, always wear gloves and a dust mask, and discard any offcuts by burying them in a hole in the ground. Don't burn them, as the smoke and ash could both be toxic.

You will probably want to fit a trimmer across the ends of the joists at this stage: screw rather than nail this in place in case there are any slight discrepancies in the cut ends of the joists.

Fixing the decking

Once the basic frame is in place and is secure, the decking boards should be fixed in exactly the same way as for a ground-level deck (see page 34). The first decking board should be placed next to the house wall, leaving a 10-mm gap for drainage (i.e. lining it up with the edge of the ledger if you left this gap when fitting this), then you can work across the deck.

If you are going to fit a balustrade, the boards should not overlap the edges of the deck — unless of course you are prepared to cut them to fit the balustrade.

Multi-level decks

Having a deck on more than one level will not only provide considerable interest, but is the ideal way of dealing with a sloping site — especially one that slopes down towards the house rather than away from it.

They may look complicated to build, but in fact they are easy: multi-level decks are simply single decks placed next to one another. It is of course possible to build one deck next to another with the two surfaces at different levels, but a multi-level deck normally involves shared supports between one level and the next.

There are three ways of doing this: sharing a bearer, sharing posts and constructing a support wall. Because all three methods mean that at least one of the deck support timbers will be carrying more load, it is important that this member should be strong enough. So you should consider going up a size — from, say, 50 × 150 mm to 50 × 200 mm — and having the supports closer together (posts at 1.5-m rather than 1.8-m intervals, for example).

The multi-level deck shown opposite is a series of ground-level decks that use shared bearers. As with steps (see page 52), the back edge of one deck uses the same support as the front edge of the next. The exposed edges (and the sides of the deck) have been finished using ribbed decking board. For details of how to add a pergola to your decking, see page 62.

Shared bearer

This is the simplest method and is particularly appropriate for ground-level decks on a sloping site, each level going up by the width of one bearer. The shared bearer is flush with the joists of the lower deck and acts as a support under the joists of the higher deck.

The lower deck joists can be secured to the shared bearer by means of joist hangers (as for a ledger beam — see page 40). The joists for the upper deck can then be laid on top of the double bearer and secured by nailing or by using galvanised brackets.

You can also use this method with an elevated deck, but the posts should be positioned under the shared bearer (i.e. no cantilever), though the lower deck can be cantilevered beyond the next line of posts if required.

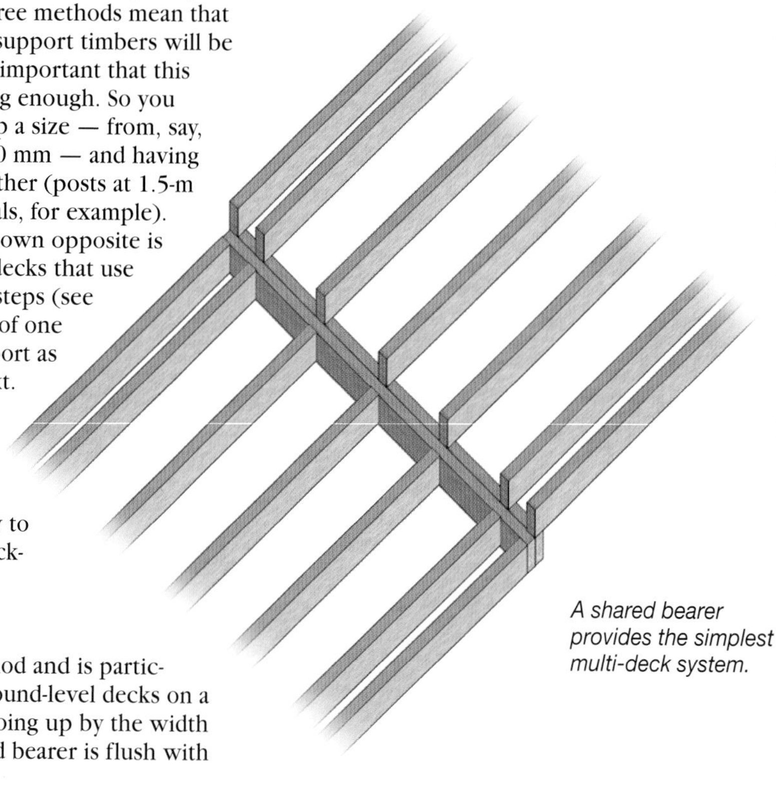

A shared bearer provides the simplest multi-deck system.

Shared posts

This method can be used with elevated decks. The posts, instead of being cut off flush with the bearers for the lower deck, continue upwards to support a second bearer for the upper deck.

The construction method is exactly the same as for an elevated deck, except for the following:

• the bearer that supports the top deck is under the edge (i.e. no cantilevering)

• you may need to mark out positions on the posts for the two sets of double bearers

• you may have to add some extra blocks around the posts to provide something to attach the decking boards at these points (if you are fitting decking boards around the posts).

An attractive alternative is to fit decking board up to the posts and then to use the posts to provide the basis for some kind of vertical cladding (e.g. tongue-and-groove or shiplap cladding).

Support wall

This method can be used with any deck, but is especially appropriate when you want to have a second platform on a ground-level deck that is higher than you could achieve with a single set of joists. This method utilises a timber framework (in effect, a tiny stud wall) built onto the back of the lower deck, providing the support for the front of the upper deck.

You'll want at least a double-thickness frame member on the lower deck to support the stud wall, which can be made from standard 50 × 100-mm (2 × 4-in) treated timber with the vertical studs at 400-mm (16-in) intervals, lining up with the joists of both lower and upper deck. The lower deck is built first, then the height of the stud wall is measured down from the proposed upper deck level (perhaps determined by a wall ledger).

As before, the lower deck joists are supported on joist hangers (or with a ground-level deck by nailing through the end trimmers) while the upper deck joists rest on the support beam — in this case the top of the stud wall. The stud

Right A multi-deck path (see page 67)

wall forms the ideal base for cladding with tongue-and-groove, shiplap or perhaps additional decking boards for a matching effect.

Curved decking

One of the big advantages of decks over hard paving is that you can form them into gentle curves that are very pleasing on the eye.

There are three ways to create a curve safely — none of them totally difficult, but all requiring quite a bit more skill and effort than a straightforward deck.

Curved decking has a very pleasing effect.

The cantilever method

This utilises the fact that decking boards can project beyond the supporting joists by a distance of a third of the joist span, i.e. up to 13 cm (5.25 in) for normal 400-mm joist spacing.

You will need to draw out the shape you want for your decking on squared graph paper, in order to calculate the way in which you need to modify the joist framework so that the

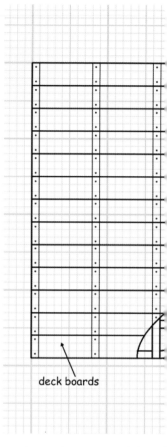

deck boards

overhangs do not exceed these limits, and also to check that no single decking board is left unsupported.

Making up a joist framework like the one shown in the drawing involves quite a lot of detailed measurement and angle cutting of the ends of the joists and the closing headers, but if you are patient and work out the angles as you go, it should be not too difficult. Make that there are no unsupported edge boards.

50

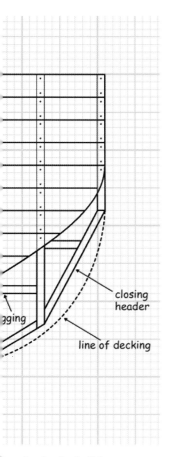

closing header

gging

line of decking

A scale plan for builidng a
urved deck using the cantilever
nethod

he kerfing method

This is a more advanced
method for creating a curve. It
basically involves bending a
piece of timber around the
required curve so that it will
support the decking boards at
the ends.

You will need to cut all the
joists to exactly the right length
and angle to suit the curve,
and you will need a helper to
assist you in bending the
timber whilst you screw it in
place on the end of every joist,
plus two extra noggings at the
sides of the deck.

The tricky part is the kerfing
process itself, whereby you
make a series of parallel saw
cuts (using a circular saw) on
the side of the timber that will
form the inside of the curve, so
that it is possible to bend it.

The circular saw must be set
to a depth of cut of three-
quarters of the thickness of the
timber — i.e. to a depth of
35 mm for 47-mm thick timber
— and saw cuts need to be
made at 25-mm (1-inch)
intervals across the width of
the board. Great care is
needed both in cutting and in
fixing. Such a task is easy for
an experienced carpenter, but
much less easy for an amateur!
The timber should also be well
soaked in water for a couple of
hours beforehand to make it
easier to bend when you start
fixing it in place.

The laminate method

This is yet another advanced
method, and again it involves
cutting all the joists to exactly
the right length for the curve
while adding extra noggings at
the sides. The laminate is built
up from layers of thin (and
therefore flexible) exterior-
grade plywood, each one glued
and screwed to the previous
one — 6-mm ($^1/_4$-in) plywood
is in fact the easiest thickness
to work with.

Mark the shape of the curve
out on the joists and cut them
to the correct length and angle
using a jigsaw. Cut the plywood into strips (plywood
comes in sheets measuring
2.4 × 1.2 m). You don't need
to wet the plywood — just
screw it to each joist in turn
with decking screws, using
quick-release clamps to hold
the strip in place.

Once the first layer is in
place, add three further layers,
smearing exterior woodworking adhesive over the surface
and adding more decking
screws, though not in the same
places as the previous ones!
You will have to make butt
joints in each layer — again,
make sure these are at different places around the rim.

Finish off with a strip of
10-mm ($^3/_8$-in) cedar-faced
plywood fixing this in the same
way as the other layers.

Finishing off

With a curved deck, you will
not be able to use a circular
saw to trim the ends of the
decking boards. A powered
jigsaw is the tool to use (see
pages 8–9), following a clearly
marked line. Do not force the
saw as this will force the blade
away from the vertical; just let
the saw do the work and let it
take as long as it takes. If you
want to add an edge, use a
strip of cedar-faced plywood.

Use a half-round rasp to
finish off the edge and remove
any splinters caused by the
sawing process.

Steps

If the 'garden' end of your deck is raised off the ground, you may well want to have steps leading down into the garden. You might also want to fit steps between two levels of decking if the height difference is too great — something that could happen on sharply sloping ground where you want to avoid each individual multi-deck being too small.

With a deck on raised ground, just one or two steps may be sufficient; with a raised deck (or a deck on sharply sloping ground), you might want to think about a full-blown staircase, with proper handrails (see page 54 for details of these).

There are two main types of steps you can have for a deck.

One is a mini-version of a multi-level deck, where the back of each step supports the front of the step behind — and, if the steps are wide, the back step uses the same support as the front of the decking. The other is a mini-staircase, where the steps are supported by side stringers (see page 54), which in turn are supported either by the lower deck or on the ground.

Multi-level steps

There are many ways of building these steps, and the method you choose will depend largely on what width of steps you require.

For really wide steps running most or all the length of the deck, you would probably choose to construct the support frame as part of the main decking just as for multi-level decks, using the posts supporting the edge of the deck to provide support for the joists under the upper step (constructed of decking boards) and resting the other end of these joists on top of the lower step.

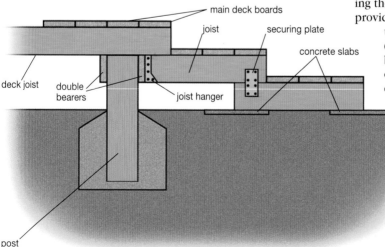

main deck boards

joist

securing plate

concrete slabs

deck joist

double bearers

joist hanger

post

The lower step obviously needs to be built first and can be supported by joists. The drawing (left) shows one possible arrangement, where the joists for the upper step are supported at one end by bearers for the main deck joists and at the other end by the joists under the lower step.

Mini-staircase

This is simply a small staircase without handrails — suitable for small rises in level only. It is constructed in much the same way as a proper staircase (see overleaf) with two stringers shaped to take the decking board steps and to fit onto the decking. If they are fitted between two decking levels, the lower deck takes the weight of the steps, but they need to be secured to the facing board of the upper deck to stop them moving or tilting. If the lower part of the steps is on the ground, the stringers should be supported on a concrete block or paving slabs laid on a sand base, as described for ground-level decking, and screwed down with angle brackets, using wallplugs.

Most decking suppliers can provide ready-made open stringers — typically with three steps — for making your own mini-staircase. All you need to do is to add decking boards for the treads; the stringers can be cut down as necessary, either to fit a specific height or if you want only two steps rather than three.

angle bracket

angle bracket

open stringer

concrete slab

Staircases

The treads of a deck staircase are contained between two side timbers — known as *stringers* — which are a fixed distance apart. A staircase will normally have a handrail, too.

There are two types of stringer — open and closed. Open stringers are formed in a zigzag shape to take the treads; closed stringers are not shaped and the treads and risers are attached to them with brackets or battens. With either stringer, vertical timbers, called *risers*, can be fitted at the back of each tread; these help support the tread above (and close off the gap), but are not essential.

The posts that support the bottom end of the handrail may support the stringers or may be attached to them while the stringers themselves rest on the ground.

Planning a staircase

There are three measurements you need to determine when designing a staircase:

- the **depth** of each step (from front to back), known technically as the *going*
- the **height** of each step — i.e. the *riser height*
- the **width** of each step (from side to side).

Tread depth

The minimum depth (or going) for a step is around 220 mm

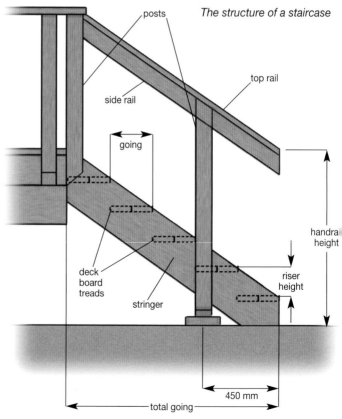

The structure of a staircase

posts

top rail

side rail

going

handrail height

deck board treads

riser height

stringer

450 mm

total going

($8^5/_8$ in), but you will probably want to use two widths of standard deckboard to make your steps, which would give a tread depth of around 285 mm (two 141-mm widths plus a 3-mm gap). On an open-tread staircase (with closed stringers), the treads can overlap, so the going is less than the tread depth.

Riser height

This is the easiest to work out: you simply divide the height of the deck from the ground by the number of steps you want, allowing for extra height created by sloping ground. The relationship between the riser height (R) and the going (G) is given by the following formula:

$$2R + G = 550 \text{ to } 700 \text{ mm}$$

So for going of 285 mm, the riser height should be between 132.5 mm and 207.5 mm and ideally around 175 mm (7 in). All steps should be the same height, so you can reckon:

- three steps for decks 396 mm to 622.5 mm (525 mm for 175-mm riser height)

- four steps for decks 528 mm to 830 mm (700 mm for 175-mm riser height)

- five steps for decks 660 mm to 1037.5 mm (875 mm for 175-mm riser height).

Note that you will need Building Regulations approval for stairs higher than 600 mm ($23^1/_2$ in), as you will always need to fit a handrail that meets the regulations.

Stair width

Stairs can be any width you like, but 900 mm (36 in) is a good choice. The minimum width for comfort is 760 mm (30 in), and stairs wider than 900 mm will need extra support in the centre.

Building a staircase

If you're using the handrail posts to support the stringers, start by marking out their position on the ground. Mark the width of the stairs on the deck and then lay a joist on top of the deck, square with the edge, and drop a plumb line to mark a point around 450 mm (18 in) closer to the deck than the end of the stairway. Dig holes (see page 42) and concrete two

posts into the ground so that their inner faces are the same distance apart as the outside of the stringers.

Unless you are using pre-cut stringers, your next task is to cut the stringers to size, using 50 × 250-mm (2 × 10-in) timber. Make a small right-angled template to represent one whole step and mark out all the treads and risers on each stringer. Cut the two ends at the correct angle and smooth off all cut edges.

Check that the stringers fit correctly and that the steps will be horizontal with the stringers in position. If you're making your own open stringers, cut the zigzag shape now; if you're having closed stringers, fit the

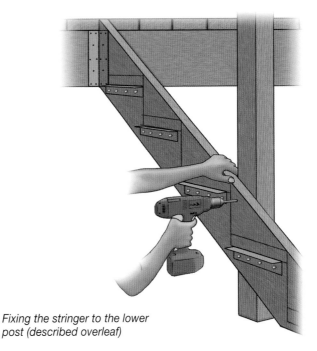

Fixing the stringer to the lower post (described overleaf)

angle brackets or timber battens that
will support the treads along the lines
you have marked for the treads. Treat
all cut edges with preservative.

You are now ready to fit the staircase. Nail or screw a large galvanised
angle bracket to the top ends of each
stringer so that it lines up with the cut
surface, and position each stringer against the
marks you made earlier on the deck before
nailing the other part of the bracket to the deck.

With the two stringers resting on the ground
slab, check that they are level with one another
(adjust the slabs if necessary), clamp the stringers to the posts and drill pilot holes through the
stringers into the posts to take three 100-mm
(4-in) securing screws (see drawing on previous
page). Remove the clamps, enlarge the holes in
the stringers and fit the securing screws. If the
stairs aren't supported by the posts, secure them
to the slab using brackets and wall anchors.

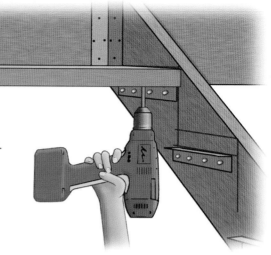

Fixing the treads to the stringers

Now cut the treads to length, cutting each
piece of deckboard so that it is exactly the
distance between the inside of closed
stringers, or overlapping the outside of
open stringers by up to 25 mm (1 in). Put
the treads in place and secure with nails or
screws: with metal brackets drill pilot
holes up from underneath (see drawing above); with timber supporting
battens (or open stringers) drill
pilot holes from above. Leave a
3-mm gap between the two
boards for drainage.

Fitting the handrail

If you are fitting proprietary
balustrading to your deck (see
page 58) you will probably want to
use matching newel posts, handrails
and balusters for the staircase handrail.
But with a simple staircase, you can make up a
handrail from standard timber lengths: the rail
itself can be a T-shape with a flat piece of timber
secured to a second piece of timber mounted
vertically between posts. The posts that support

*Measure up carefully before
fitting the handrails to the posts.*

...he staircase at the bottom also form ...he support for the handrail.

Start the handrail by fitting square ...osts to the deck edge joist, using ...0-mm (3/8-in) coach bolts. The ...eight of the rail should be around ...00 mm (36 in) above the deck, so ...he upper posts will need to be this length plus the whole thickness of the deck joist plus decking boards). Measure the final ...eight exactly and transfer this measurement ...o the lower posts.

The side rails are made from 50 × 100-mm ...imbers, and these should first be clamped to ...he post so that the cutting lines can be ...narked on both the posts and the rails — ...tand back and check by eye that the rails are ...t the correct angle before making the marks ...see drawing below left). Cut both rail and ...ost to shape, treat all cut ends with preserva-...ive and secure the rails to the posts.

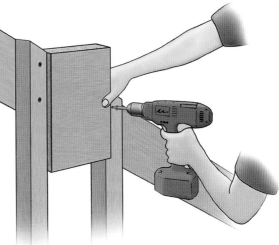

Use a spacer to help position the balusters.

Now mark out the lengths of all the balusters ...hat can be made from 38-mm ($1^1/_2$-in) or 50-mm ...2-in) square timber. These can be fitted to the ...utside of the side rail and the stringers, going ...bout halfway down the stringers for neatness. ...he balusters should be positioned no more ...han 100 mm apart, so use a spacer block made ...rom an offcut to achieve this (see drawing ...bove right); you might need to adjust the spacer ...o get equal spacing). Cut the balusters to the ...orrect length and angle, and screw them to the ...ide rails and stringers, after drilling holes.

Finish off by fitting the main handrails, which ...an be made from 100 × 25-mm (4 × 1-in) ...imber and are simply positioned over the side ...ails, overlapping so that they cover the tops of ...he balusters (see drawing). Mark and cut the ...handrails to the correct size and shape — they ...will need to be angled at the top, but should be ...left square at the bottom, where they protrude ...beyond the post. Use an electric sander to ...make the handrails really smooth and to ...round off all the corners before screwing ...them in place. Fill the screw holes with ...exterior wood filler for neatness.

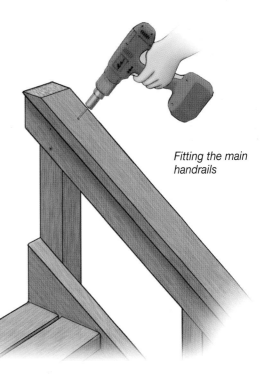

Fitting the main handrails

Balustrades

A balustrade around your deck will not only make it safer to use (handrails are compulsory on decks over 600 mm high), but will enhance its appearance, giving it a more complete look. Remember that the balustrade is the first part of the deck that anyone will see, so it needs to complement the structure. Bear in mind too that it may well get in the way of your view when you are sitting on the deck.

There are three main types of balustrade:

• a proprietary post-and-baluster system, perhaps using ornate newel posts, caps and turned balusters

• a proprietary post-and-panel-system, where individual balusters are replaced by a series of decorative panels

• a home-made system, again using posts, but with your own balustrade.

A staircase to a high-level deck, made using the same components as proprietary balustrading

A proprietary balustrade with 'Colonial' balusters

Planning balustrading

The normal height for a balustrade on a low-level deck is 900 mm ($35^1/_2$ in), but for higher decks (where you must conform to Building Regulations), you will need a taller balustrade. So it can be effective as a guard rail, the vertical balusters should not leave gaps of 100 mm or more. Horizontal rails, although attractive, should not be used as they provide an inviting climbing frame for young children. Posts are needed at regular intervals to support the balustrade — certainly no less than one every 1.8 m (6 ft) and preferably one every 1.2 m (4 ft).

If the support posts for a raised deck (or a deck on sloping ground) are at the edge of the decking, these can used (provided they haven't been cut off!) to support the balustrade. Alternatively, posts can be attached to the decking support frame — i.e. to the joists or to a closing trimmer fitted across the ends of the joists.

Posts can be attached to the inside or the outside of the joists, and can be either fitted whole (using long coach bolts right through the post and the joist) or lapped, so that some the post's thickness is cut away to form a rebate, and so that the balustrade itself is more directly above the edge of the decking. Balustrade posts should be fitted before the final decking boards are laid so that, if necessary, the decking can be fitted around them. You need to think about balustrading at the deck planning stage.

Proprietary post and baluster

Most suppliers of decking will have newel posts and balusters in their range — perhaps just one style, perhaps several.

The style illustrated here is known as 'Colonial' and uses a shaped newel post and a turned baluster. Cleverly, only one type of rail is used to support the balusters — inverted at the bottom and right way up at the top. Finally, a third rail is fitted over the top rail in order to conceal the screw heads that fix it to the balusters. The rails are attached to the posts by a special fixing system. The whole balustrade (posts, rails and balusters) should be assembled on a flat surface (the garage floor is ideal) before being offered up to the decking.

Cut the top and bottom rails to length, if necessary, so that they fit

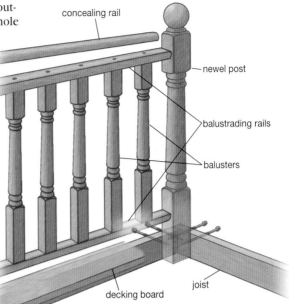

concealing rail

newel post

balustrading rails

balusters

joist

decking board

The construction of a 'Colonial' balustrade

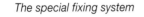

The special fixing system

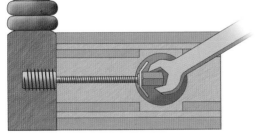

between the posts and drill holes in the ends of the rails to take the special fixing. Mark the position of the rails on the posts so that the bottom rail is around 75 mm (3 in) above the finished deck and drill holes in the posts to take the other half of the special fixing. Secure the top and bottom rails to the posts.

Mark the baluster positions at about 120-mm intervals, so that the maximum gap between the balusters at any point is 100 mm — though you may want to reduce this to get equal spacing. Screw the spindles to both the top and bottom rails, using 63-mm ($2^1/_2$-in) screws and screw the covering rail in place over the top rail, using screws up through the top rail.

With a helper holding the balustrade in place, the newel posts can now be attached to the decking joists, preferably to a double-height joist so that the first 300 mm (12 in) of the post is secured — for ground-level decks, it may be necessary to concrete the bottom part of the post into the ground.

Above *A balustrade with Chippendale panels*

Below *A drawing of a Sunburst panel showing where the screws should go in*

Proprietary post and panel

The advantage of using balustrading panels is that you don't have to fix individual balusters. The disadvantage is that you may need more posts, as the panels are only around 110 cm long (the ones shown here are 117 cm long and 77 cm high) — unless you also fit balusters either side, which is something you might have to do if your deck size is not an exact multiple of panel widths.

The panels are designed to be used with top and bottom rails, which are secured to the posts using either galvanised L-brackets or screws angled through the rails into the posts, and which are secured to the panels with more screws going from the panel into the rail to leave the top surface clear of screw holes (as in the Sunburst example on the left).

The recommended method of fixing the panels is to use two spacer blocks to position the bottom rail 75-100 mm off the deck surface — a gap that is generally known as the *sweep space*.

Home-made balustrade

The disadvantage of using the decking support posts as supports for a balustrade is that they may not be very attractive. You can, however, buy proper newel posts separately, plus a selection of rails and balusters, so that you can make up your own balustrading.

The one shown here uses lightly shaped newel posts screwed to the trimmers or joists (the posts have been given a small rebate of 21 mm). The handrail is held to the posts with screws driven up at an angle through the ends, and the individual balusters (shaped at the bottom) are secured to the rail with angled screws and to the deck with nails directly into the deck joists.

Note that with this kind of balustrading it is not quite so easy to sweep the deck clean.

Using decking posts

One effective way of using the decking support posts to support a handrail and balusters is to cut the post so that it fits underneath the handrail. Two lengths of handrail can be mitred (cut at 45 degress) where they meet over the posts.

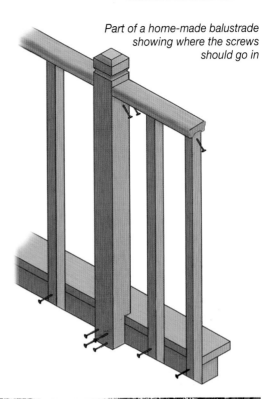

Part of a home-made balustrade showing where the screws should go in

A multi-level path with a home-made balustrade

Adding a pergola

A pergola is a really attractive garden feature and provides a useful frame for hanging things on — lights, planting baskets and so on — as well as a frame up which plants can grow. If you add a pergola to a ground-level deck, the plants can provide some shade in the summer — but you normally need to think about the pergola at the planning stage, rather than trying to add it afterwards.

Pergola basics

A pergola is a really simple construction and really consists of just three main components:

• posts to support the structure

• cross-beams supported by the posts

• rafters supported by the cross-beams.

However, it may also have corner pieces attached to the posts to provide additional support to both cross-beams and rafters.

So it's a bit like a high-level deck without the deckboards, though it has only to carry its own weight, not the weight of people and furniture.

The other main difference is that the posts used for constructing a pergola — typically at a height of 2.1 m (7 ft) off the ground — are normally slotted to take the cross-beams, and the rafters may be slotted to fit over the cross-beams. As you can see from the photograph, the cross-beams project beyond the posts and the rafters project beyond the cross-beams. Both are of the same size of timber (50 × 100 mm) and both traditionally have shaped ends, but you can buy timbers with both ends square (like those used in decking) or with just one end square (where one cross-beam of the pergola is fixed to the house).

You can buy pre-slotted posts for use with ground-level decks. With an elevated deck you should use longer plain posts (which can also support the deck) and cut your own slots.

A ground-level deck with a pergola and a balustrade

If you are using pre-slotted rafters, the spacing of the posts and the crossbeams is crucial and therefore to be built into the design of the deck.

The posts for a pergola are concreted into the ground in the same way as described for a raised deck on page 42 — they simply pass through the deck with the deckboards cut to fit around them. If you are using plain posts to support both a raised deck and a pergola above it, make sure the slots are cut in the posts before you concrete them into the ground — unless you are using twin cross-beams attached either side of the rafter as shown in the photograph on page 47.

Provided you have the posts in the correct places with the slots correctly aligned, then constructing a pergola with pre-cut components is easy: you just slot it together. The components are designed to fit fairly tightly, so you may need a mallet (or a club hammer and a protective piece of wood) to join the parts together.

To secure cross-beams to posts, hammer galvanised nails into the cross-beam from each side of the post. To secure slotted rafters to the cross-beams, nail down through each rafter at each junction. Non-slotted rafters are held by pergola brackets — first nailed down to the cross-beam and then to the rafters after they have been laid in the brackets. Whichever method you use, make sure the rafters are equally spaced.

With large pergolas, finish off by nailing supporting corner pieces (already cut to the correct angles at the ends) onto the posts, and to the rafter and cross-beam that pass over each post.

You can also add shaped trellis panels to a pergola to provide additional support for plants — or just for the effect it creates.

Building a pergola

Set out the position of the posts when setting out the main deck, and dig holes for concreting them into the ground (see page 42 for details). If the posts are slotted, you will want to make sure that that they are in line and that the slots are all facing the correct way. Check, too, that the distance between the post centres matches the slots in pre-slotted rafters. With non-slotted rafters, you can either cut your own slots to suit the cross-beam spacing later, or simply lay the rafters on top of the posts, secured by pergola brackets. If you want to combine the pergola with a balustrade (see page 58), you may need some additional posts at one or more edges of the deck.

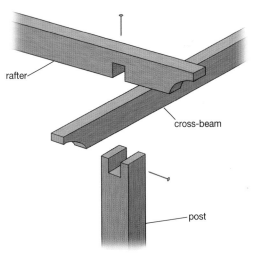

rafter

cross-beam

post

Provided the posts are exactly in place, nailing the cross-beams and rafters is very straightforward.

63

Adding a planter

There are several ways you can add plants to your deck, from simple small plastic or terra-cotta plant pots to full-blown planters. The planter shown in the photograph is a clever way of improving the look of broad steps, using the same materials as the surrounding decking so that it blends in.

Planter basics

Planters can be put in several places on the deck: small planters can be put on top of the finished deck or built into wide balustrades; larger ones can be built on the side of the deck or within the main deck area itself.

For planters within decks, it will normally be best if some of the planter is below the surface and some above — so what you are doing is in effect to make an inset box.

This box should ideally be constructed from exterior-grade plywood, with holes drilled in the bottom for drainage.

The box can be supported in one of several ways:

- directly on the decking boards

- on the joists supporting the decking boards (with the boards fitted around it)

- on timbers laid directly on the ground (for an inset box on a ground-level deck)

- by means of timbers joined to the main deck frame (for an inset box on an elevated deck).

An inset box can be additionally secured at the sides to the joists that support the decking. Decking boards secured to the top of the box can be used to make a concealing frame. For neatness, this frame can be mitred (cut at 45 degrees) at the corners.

You could use the box to put other containers in, which would allow plant displays to be changed at regular intervals — but if it is to be filled with earth, it will need to be lined.

The material used for lining ponds is ideal for this purpose, but you should always puncture holes in it to match the drainage holes in the box. The framing material can then be used to conceal the edges of the box.

The same method of construction can also be used to create a children's sandpit in a deck — but in this case you would want the top of the sunken box to be flush with the deck surface, and you would need to ensure that the edges of the surrounding deck are smooth rather than sharp. Remember to keep the drainage holes sufficiently small to prevent sand being washed out after rain.

Above *A planter can be incorporated into most decking designs.*

Adding a water feature

There is nothing quite like the sound and look of running water to give an air of peacefulness and relaxation which may just fit with all your thinking behind having a deck in the first place. It's easier than you may think to install one.

About water features

We're not talking about a full-blown pond here, but rather a self-contained feature with an electric pump inside that drives water down a small waterfall or operates a small fountain. You will find several versions of these self-contained water features in places like garden centres (look in specialised water garden centres as well), including artificial millstones, pebble ponds, wishing wells, bubbling urns and lots of other ideas.

What they all have in common is that no external water supply is needed as the same water is circulated and only needs to be topped up to make up for evaporation losses. No installation is required as such (the whole water feature simply sits on a suitable surface), unless you need to provide your own container or want to construct a matching frame, like the hexagonal frame shown here made from decking boards, but the pump will require an electrical supply.

This can be a mains or a low-voltage supply. It could even be a solar-powered supply with no additional wiring needed; the water feature will drive itself whenever the sun gives enough power. (Don't be too carried away: the feature may not work after several dull days and may turn itself on on a sunny day when you don't want it!)

A deck next to the house provides the ideal route for a mains supply: cable can be run in a conduit attached to the frame of the decking (having been led out through a hole in the house wall), the flex from the feature can be passed unobtrusively down through the decking to join up with the supply underneath in a waterproof junction box. However, you might want to have an electrician install the outside part of the circuit for you.

A low-voltage pump is an even better choice: a transformer is connected to the mains inside the house and a low-voltage cable (typically 24V) run to the position of the water feature (again running the wire under the decking would be ideal).

It is essential to keep the feature fully topped up with water (to avoid the pump running dry), and you will probably want to disconnect the pump and store it inside during the winter.

Below *A water feature brings a sense of peace and relaxation.*

Decking for paths

If you have a deck in your garden, the same materials can be used to create pathways within the garden, leading from the deck. Not only does this provide cohesion between deck and garden, but it also provides a surface that is comfortable to walk on and easy to keep clean.

How to use decking for paths

A decking path can be made in exactly the same way as a ground-level deck — that is, decking boards laid on a simple timber framework

resting directly on the ground, or preferably on paving slabs laid on a sand base. You should be able to manage with smaller timbers than you would use for a full-size deck — perhaps 50 × 100 mm rather than 50 × 150 mm — but you will need to take care to get the framework flat and level (or perhaps with a slight slope across the path so that water falls off to one side).

For a wide path like the one shown in the photograph below, you will need a framework of three joists — one on either side and one

running down the middle, with the joists spaced by noggings running at right angles. You will need to join some of the joists end-to-end, which you can manage by bolting a length of timber on the inside of the joining joists, over-lapping each one by around 300 mm (1 ft). Make sure the framework is secure and level before nailing or screwing down the decking boards as for a normal deck.

An angled path

The narrow 484-mm (19-in) path in the photo on the right has been created using the medium size of the pre-cut shapes sold for creating octagons (see panel below). The 22.5° angle provides a gentle corner and the steps have been created by securing the front edge of one piece over the top of the back edge of another.

A free-standing octagon

The pre-cut decking shapes used to create the octagon on the right can be used for a multitude of designs, includ-ing the meandering path described in the panel above.

There are three sizes available — small, medium and large — and you need eight of each size to make the full octagon. Additional small pieces have been interlocked to create the small path leading off to the right. Octagons like this can be used either as a garden centrepiece (as here) or as the floor for a greenhouse or summer house.

Decking treatments

There are several different treatments you can apply to a deck to make it look good — and to keep it looking good. Decking treatments break down into three groups:

- treatments to be applied before installation
- treatments to be applied after installation
- treatments for maintaining the deck in the longer term.

Initial treatments

The main initial treatment is the timber preservative you must use on any cut timber (or on all the timber if it hasn't been pre-treated, as it should have been). When you cut preservative-treated timber, you expose areas which the pressure-impregnation may not have reached completely, so you need to apply extra preservative to these areas. Most decking suppliers have their own preservative treatment for this purpose, which you can buy at the same time as you buy the decking. Read the instructions carefully to see what safety precautions are necessary when you apply the preservative.

wood unfinished will make it more difficult to clean and it will weather more quickly.

A clear water repellent (deck seal) is the simplest option: it won't stop the greying process, but it will keep water out of the deck timber and prevent algal growth on the surface of the deck.

Coloured deck stains are the best way of preventing the wood going grey and are available in a range of natural wood colours and pastel shades. Deck stains also contain water repellents and anti-fungal agents, and are available in both heavy-duty (high-build) and standard-duty (low-build) versions.

A decking oil provides an attractive, hard-wearing and durable finish. Applied by brush, it provides protection against the weather — including filters to protect against the effects of UV light — and it contains preservatives.

Paint, which sits on the surface rather than penetrating the wood as a stain does, is a somewhat drastic way to treat a deck — unless you are using inferior-quality wood. Although it may look good at first, an exterior paint applied to a deck will quickly wear in areas where furniture is used or there is a lot of walking, thus leading to a very uneven appearance. The deck will need to be re-painted frequently to keep it looking good.

Above *This deck has been stained with a light colour that contrasts well with the blue furniture.*

Left *There is a vast range of specialist decking treatments available — this photo shows those on offer from one company alone.*

Right *Both deck and steps here have been treated with decking oil.*

Deck finishes

There are four main types of deck finish which you can apply to your deck to change its appearance: water seals, stains, oils and paints.

You could of course just leave the deck in its unfinished state and allow it to weather naturally — in time all wood goes grey — but leaving

Above *The deck and surrounding pergola have been given a strong blue colour for a total contrast with the pine furniture.*

Right *Both the decking and the furniture have been treated with an attractive cedar decking stain.*

Deck maintenance

However well you have treated your deck in the first place, it will inevitably get dirty. There may be growth of algae on the surface and the original treatment may have worn away so that it needs replacing.

All decks should be brushed regularly to remove surface dirt — and if they are really dirty, they should be hosed down with water. A high-pressure sprayer is a good way to remove engrained dirt, but should not be used on painted decks as it could cause the paint to lift.

You can buy specialised deck cleaners that contain detergents to remove dirt and grease, plus chemicals to kill algae and mould while at the same time sterilising the deck surface to prevent re-growth. Check the instructions carefully to see what safety precautions are necessary for their application.

Right Four different finishes are shown in this picture, wIth decking and balustrading in seaport blue and American mahogany, and garden furniture in teak and topiary green.

Applying a deck stain

Although decking stains contain a certain amount of preservative, they should not be used on untreated timber — so the first task with untreated timber is to apply an appropriate preservative and leave this to dry for at least 48 hours before applying the treatment.

All surfaces that are to be treated with the stain should be clean, dry and free of any resins or oils that could affect the product's performance. New wood can be simply wiped with white spirit once all dirt and dust has been

removed; weathered wood should be sanded back to clear new wood; painted or varnished wood should be stripped or sanded.

The stain itself should be applied by brush, and two or three coats may be necessary, depending on the final colour you want to achieve. You will need to allow 24 hours between coats — and a few days before the deck can be fully used again.

Decking ideas

Before settling on the design for your deck, it's a good idea to look at as many different designs as you can. You could discover features you might never have thought of — or thought possible. Or you might find new and different ways of doing things, or perhaps even find solutions to apparently intractable problems.

The photographs on these pages — plus yet more on the opening and closing pages of this book — should provide you with some useful ideas for designs you might adopt.

Play space (right)
A deck could be the ideal place for children to play safely, and where you can keep an eye on them. A shallow, self-draining, sandpit set into the deck adds to the fun.

Outdoor dining room
The balustrading on this good-looking deck fits around a rockery and provides a screen between the barbecue and the dining area. A tree provides excellent shade at one end of the deck, and the whole provides a link between house and garden.

Imposing approach (above)

Decking — here fitted with balustrading — can provide an impressive pathway and approach to the house. To add interest, the decking boards have been laid at a slight angle.

Keeping it safe

Balustrading added to a deck will not only enhance its appearance (as on the lowest of these multi-level decks) but is also necessary for safety (as in the case of the highest deck).

More decking ideas overleaf ...

Well thought out (above)

This deck has been beautifully designed to create a world of its own. On three levels, with a stunning pergola as a backdrop, it catches the sun and is an easy-to-maintain plant paradise.

Instant deck

To provide an attractive and stable decking area, these pre-constructed decking squares, complete with integral battens, can be laid quickly and easily directly over most surfaces.

Combined effects (right)

There's no reason why you should have to choose between only decking and only paving materials — you can have both! This delightful arrangement uses shallow decking steps, stained in contrasting colours, leading up to the main deck and interspersed with pebbles and rock plants. The idea could be extended to include a water feature within the pebbles.

Mediterranean glory

This spectacular multi-level deck is built around a well-stocked pool, backed by a superb arbour and set off with several planters. The decking boards, laid in contrasting patterns, have been finished with decking oil.

Glossary

Aggregate: small stones used for making concrete (with cement, sand and water)

Arbour: a garden structure, usually including an arch and a seat

Balustrade: a vertical structure added to edge of deck or stairway, consisting of posts, rails and balusters (banisters)

Batten: generic term for straight piece of timber

Batter boards: T-shapes used for setting out decking

Bearer: a timber used to support joists (normally attached to posts)

Builder's square: three pieces of timber in the ratio 3:4:5 joined together to form a right angle

Cantilever: the unsupported length of timber that projects from the last support

CCA (chromated copper arsenate): a preservative used for treating deck timbers

Clearance hole: a small hole drilled for a screw to pass through

Conduit: metal or plastic tubing or channelling used for running electric cable safely

Fascia: a decorative finishing board

Flashing: soft metal (zinc or lead) strips used for weatherproofing joins in buildings

Galvanised: steel or iron coated with zinc to prevent it rusting

Going: the distance from the front to the back of a step

Colonial splendour evoking the days of British Empire — a covered deck, fitted with a balustrade and a roof covering, provides a perfect place to while away summer evenings.

Joist: a timber support for deck boards

Ledger: a bearer attached to a house wall (also known as wallplate)

MDF (medium-density fibreboard): a board material with a smooth finish and even consistency

Newel: the post at the top and bottom of a staircase

Nogging: a short length of timber fitted between joists to add strengthening

Pilot hole: a small hole drilled to guide screw or nail

Planter: a container holding soil and/or compost for plants

Pressure treatment: the way timber is treated with preservative, forcing preservative into the grain

Reeding: grooving or channelling in the underside of deck boards designed to provide ventilation and aid drainage.

Risers: the vertical parts of a staircase fitted between the treads

Shiplap: a type of timber cladding where one piece overlaps the next

Straight-edge: a piece of metal or timber with at least one straight edge, used for marking out or guiding a saw

Stringers: the timbers used to form the sides of a staircase

Stud: vertical timber used in the framework for a partition wall

Template: a shaped pattern used for cutting out pieces (e.g. of timber)

Tongue-and-groove: a type of timber cladding where one piece slots into the next

Treads: the horizontal parts of a staircase

Trimmer: closing timber used across the ends of joists

Wallplate *see* **Ledger**

Decking suppliers

Board Walk

0870 241 1250
www.board-walk.co.uk

As part of a long-established company (The Loft Shop) that has been distributing wood products for over 70 years, Board Walk is able to offer all the experience, know-how, advice and support you may need to add a deck to your home, as well as being able to provide all the components. All products available for delivery from stock, in some cases guaranteed next day. Three shops in London.

Free brochure available together with an installation guide (£5).

Richard Burbidge

01691 678201 (brochure/stockists)
01691 678212 (technical helpline)
www.richardburbidge.co.uk

The UK's leading supplier of decorative timber products, famous for their DIY balustrading and mouldings. A wide range of decking products available throughout the UK.

Can provide a free leaflet, an installation video (£5.99) and a comprehensive 64-page A4 book (*Decking – the Essential Guide*, £5.99) with 12 deck designs.

Forest Garden

01886 812451
www.forestgarden.co.uk

The UK's leading supplier of timber products for the garden, from arbours and arches to bridges, fencing, garden buildings, pergolas, planters, screens and trellis — and, of course, decking. Decking and other products widely available throughout the UK from timber merchants, garden centres and the like.

Can provide a free catalogue and leaflet — *How to Build a Deck*.

This deck uses several matching garden structures to provide a wondrous plant display: a pergola with lattice inserts (for added stability), fence panels, two designs of free-standing planter, a Cooper's tub and a flowerbed contained by log roll. The pergola provides shade as well as plant support.

Timber Decking Association

01977 712718

www.tda.org.uk

The Timber Decking Association (TDA) is an organisation of companies who have joined forces to help home-owners and design professionals to source and create high-quality and performance timber decks.

The TDA has established best practice design and installation procedures, and also operates the Deck Mark™ quality-assurance scheme for the materials used in deck construction or the quality of design and installation companies. It also operates an independent insurance warranty scheme.

Can provide a free leaflet (*An Introduction to Creating Quality Decks*) and the *Timber Decking Manual* (£29.99) — best-practice guide and installation guide for professionals — as well as a list of quality-assessed suppliers.

Wickes Home Improvement Centres

0500 300 328

www.wickes.co.uk

A major DIY retailer with over 130 stores in the UK, Wickes prides itself on stocking everything you need to complete your outdoor projects.

A product booklet is available in-store, along with the free *Good Idea Leaflet No 15* (Wickes Timber Decking and Pergolas) and decking brochure: *Decking - a modern garden alternative.*

Decking treatments

Cuprinol: 01753 877930; **www.cuprinol.co.uk**

Ronseal: 0114 246 7171; **www.ronseal.co.uk**

Liberon: 01797 367555 (no website)

Index